T0114263

The Key to our Soul Internet

Stanley Chair

Order this book online at www.trafford.com
or email orders@trafford.com

Most Trafford titles are also available at major online book retailers.

Printed in the United States of America.

ISBN: 978-1-4120-8961-6 (sc)

Trafford rev. 04/09/2011

 www.trafford.com

North America & international
toll-free: 1 888 232 4444 (USA & Canada)
phone: 250 383 6864 • fax: 812 355 4082

Acknowledgement and Dedication

An adage of 'no man is an island' is perfectly illustrated when work of writers are analyzed by their peers. It is relevant that some authors are stronger in certain areas than others and it's always easier to perceive the smudges on someone else's brainchild then it is our own. Only when a group meets to review presentations of others; do we then become aware of anomalies that may have been overlooked. It is imperative that egos must be subdued before corrections are considered. As with all else in the universe, knowledge evolves and these sessions give positive boosts to literary compositions.

I've been fortunate to be associated with the talent and expertise of individuals that have contributed significantly to this manuscript's finish.

The majority of them were professional teachers at one time and many have published works to their credit. My many thanks go to the people of this group whose last names will only be initialed. They will know why this is done and still recognize their affiliation. Because of highly evolved contents in the book, they will be relieved of the pressure to explain certain subjects that is beyond the grasp of those who have not studied them.

Evelyn S. - retired teacher – creator of beautiful poetry and stories.

Nyla N. - a retired teacher – author of humorous short stories.

Wanda D. - a teacher and writer with unusual depth of perception.

Roger M. - excellent writer with dozens of published articles.

Benn L. – a retired teacher - now working on his second book.

Norman D. - retired teacher – published poet.

James D. - retired teacher - poet - astute scholar of academia.

Dedication

This manuscript is dedicated to my two sons, my daughter, their children and those to be. I've had wonderful rapport and family love with them throughout my life and consider myself the luckiest of people.

- Stanley Chair -

PROLOGUE

(Degrees are given on the expertise for memorizing thoughts of others)

This manuscript deals with our world's social problems and presents factual reasons why the various methods to solve them engender little success. We wander around on this planet not knowing specifically what our purpose in this life is all about. Psychologically insecure and short on personal knowledge we are prone to adopt the views of others.

Struggling with our humanity, most of us conclude that we have dual bodies but find it difficult to harmonize the physical and spiritual aspects into an agreeable lock. The confusion that ensues makes for a myriad of misconceptions and conclusions. This stretches across all academic and professional lines, where expertise in studied principles are given degrees for the profundity of memorizing someone else's thoughts. Practitioners thereof, are then surveyed as the highest source of wisdom and the actual validity of presumed truths are seldom questioned. These attitudes produce feedbacks that impede self-thought and the impetus to search for other alternatives.

With all of the supposed intelligence manufactured by institutions of learning in the past century, why do we still find ourselves in repeated states of jeopardy?

Unless a diploma is acquired the common sense of laymen have little chance of being heard or published in our tinseled world of illusions. So, for what it is worth, an effort is made here to set forth logical viewpoints as far removed as possible from traditional ethnics, religions, politics, etc. Until our programmed minds can discard the illusion of complete authenticity of written words and adjust to factual thinking there can be little social progress; for much of the previous data 'downloaded' in our computer minds have a tendency to be very questionable.

Condensing and reducing detail in this manuscript give readers a chance to use analytical reasoning and becoming mentally involved.

A

Words lose import unless stimuli of recipient viewpoints become active parts in a presentation. Though clichés as statements of fact is frowned upon, it does save time and space when used in an unbiased descriptive manner. Vivid comparisons can simplify explanations and make reading efforts more enjoyable. This is sometimes so for metaphors as well.

Most referrals are senseless however, for ironically they too would have to be researched in determining their reliability. This may pyramid to great lengths with many involved writers before the base source is reached. If original data proves negative then repetition only compounds the error. Tracing a concept or quote to end limits, may reveal that the original author was 'dropped on its head when a baby;' unquote. Then again most referrals are linked to older data whereas, newer discoveries are usually far more accurate and accountable. Taking a look at computer technology we begin to realize how fast things can change.

It is hoped that this manuscript will inspire readers to use syllogistic reasoning (objective, subjective and deductive) creatively, so it too, may contribute to the positive influence of universal thought. Esoteric logic becomes 'speed bumps' to objective minds requiring them to slow down and begin relative thinking. Habitual mind patterns must first be altered so new knowledge and instantaneous enlightenment is apt to be a rarity. Many lessons we have yet to learn but with reasonable effort most are both bearable and solvable. The practice of patience and communication with the inner self will create for us a more meaningful existence. If there is a humble desire for the truth, it will be revealed to us when we are best prepared to cope with it. The majority of people want to believe in a First Cause or Divine Overseer, for logic tells us that something cannot be made from nothing and we like to believe that some higher intelligence was responsible for designing and creating the laws which govern nature and the rest of our beautiful universe.

B

Our security is always crying in desperation for explanations to unanswered questions about life and to fill this void we then settle for illusionary concepts of traditional thought.

If we knew the truth of all things, where then would our progress begin? Was certain knowledge deliberately withheld from us so that we may continue to wonder and contemplate; thus allowing our thinking capacity to grow and evolve?

A lack of relative perception was sensed in the Iliad, compared to a later work of the Odyssey. If Homer authored both books, did he evolve in consciousness during the time span between them? This is unlikely and it would be more logical that the later work was authored by another person; quite possibly a woman. Intuitiveness is another development of consciousness and this strength seems predominant in women, that may at times give them a mental edge over men.

Judging from past actions of humans, we may still be in an embryo stage of mental development.

The word 'divine' is often used throughout the manuscript because it is more commonly understood, however, the more accurate reference of 'cosmic' will be introduced from time to time for it encompasses an entire essence of known and unknown forces that completes the universe. Humans still cling to the primitive individuality of spiritual beings and the variety involved points to the fact that we invent our own gods and demons. It is not easy to admit but isn't this a throwback to superstitions of pagan ancestors? For this reason, the word 'cosmic' broadens the scope of our awareness that is necessary if we are to grow in proportion to perception of the variables in an esoteric consciousness. A deterrent to any new knowledge is change and new data cannot be forced on anyone who is not prepared to understand it. Unless, we are curious enough and not fearful to open a door to and see what's on the other side, as it were, there is really no hope of us reaching a higher plateau of awareness.

C

Two of the most consistent laws of the universe are those of change along with cause and effect. Change is repugnant to insecure people for it affects their habitual patterns of behavior and they must learn all over again. This disturbs them most when science comes along and disturbs their ingrained concepts of security that they believe are 'inscribed in stone' forever. All that is demonstrated in nature is proof that everything evolves with growth whether thought, physical or organically inclined.

It can also be logically concluded that creation of the universe is the effect of a first cause. What or whom that first cause is will undoubtedly remain a mystery while we remain in our present dimension. Instilled fear with threats of revenge from illusionary gods if we don't please them are the same rhetoric we find in pagan superstitions thousands of years ago. The only difference is the 'fancier outer garments' that are worn to make a bigger impression. Over the years, Christian writer imaginations have run amok, even increasing the brutal revenge supposedly condoned by their supernatural beings. There is no empirical proof that a god ever said a word but authors continue to lie about the immutable word of god or of them being divinely inspired of which there is also no proof. The fears were concocted for power and control of the unschooled masses.

To embrace our faith with rhetoric of traditional or orthodox thought we are prone to repeat their mistakes even to that of killing one another. Proof or truth is generally ignored and seldom is it realized that we are not highly civilized and haven't evolved much beyond animal instincts or laws the jungle. All prayers and clichés of God bless us appear as mere trash talk if we cannot find cosmic love in our soul and thereby manifest the peace therein. Only by negative comparisons can we reach beneficial conclusions. Can we fear and still communicate with our inner self? Is it possible for cosmic love to grow in our hearts while there is still hate in our minds? These questions will be discussed later.

THE KEY TO OUR SOUL INTERNET

Table of Contents

FOREWORD

(As communication with soul grows, intuitive wisdom will be unveiled)

As light beings, we have entered bodies in this dimension to take our place in its sun and work out experiences that are intended as lessons for our progress. Over the ages, myths have dominated our lives with fear and social pressures. Controlled thought patterns restrict rationale and narrows our perspectives. This manuscript will attempt to counteract negative influence by bringing together collective information relative to personal growth and illumination. Only after fear is removed, can we find the peace within and begin to enjoy that universal love.

Like computers, if minds are programmed erroneously, final results will also be flawed. Mere assumptions have little value in our data bank and if not deleted they will act like a mental virus. As communication with the inner self grows, intuitive wisdom will be unveiled. Knowledge of past, present and future can be tapped from cosmic records for we are one in essence with all of creation. Thus, the term 'ever present now' is often used but it's far too difficult to understand for most and must not be of concern at this phase in our progress. We have enough problems comprehending simpler things and the necessity of peaceful co-existence with others. When something can't be determined objectively, it should be transferred to the subconscious by meditation and given time for the data to be processed through the Soul's Internet, as it were. Third eye development and the quality of its perception will also be enhanced the more this is repeated. We must be humble and in control of the egos before vibrations can be raised in rapport with our true being.

Meditation can tap into otherwise hidden data that can be of great benefit to us. To some extent we have the inherent power to be our own 'crystal ball'. It is not surprising for an adept to receive answers from within that surpasses any relative data obtained by conventional means. Thus it was with Einstein, De Vinci and other great minds throughout history.

As our wisdom grows to clarify new knowledge, fear can no longer hold us captive and we shall be free to walk in our own light.

Certain thought or projected information here may be uncomfortable to many at first but don't be dismayed or judgmental until the complete book is read. Let the data rest on our mental shelves for a time, neither accepting nor rejecting it. Old concepts 'die hard ' and like the habitual use of drugs they can't be discarded immediately without a withdrawal effect. When our psyche is mentally prepared to review the contents objectively, long sought answers will spring forth, many from the most unlikely sources. As this enlightenment continues, we will experience a great new feeling of peace and confidence. Being as we are of cosmic origin, truths that emanate from this bond cannot be claimed as our own.

To many, answers that come through the higher self will be recognized immediately, while with others it may take some time. There is no time or limits in the cosmic, however, because this is merely a human illusion. Aspects of truth will be revealed when we have earned their recognition. Diligent study of esoteric knowledge may not only improve our lives but can also lead to refining portions of everything we read and that would include this manuscript as well, for light of truth is always progressive. The separate discourses contained herein are so arranged to compliment each other. Unless psychology or researching religions have been heavy subjects of study, it may be best to limit the discourses we read per day. This is important, for it gives us time to meditate and do some bonding on its contents. Reviewing a previous chapter may also be helpful so that relative factors can be established. The results may be worth the effort for we will begin to know ourselves better and realize the purpose and responsibilities of our sojourn in this life. With each progressive step we take, perception of our ties to the beautiful universe becomes more acute. The gift of universal love has been installed in each soul and the awareness of this is very beneficial to us but it doesn't stop there.

This love is reciprocal in nature and must be shared and reflected to reap its full reward. Without love a newborn baby will wither and die; this holds true for other aspects of life also. This factor also influences the life span of nations and civilizations; when government leaders become selfish and corrupt, the downfall of that country is eminent; no matter how great they may appear at the moment. We live under an immutable law of cause and effect and only from this position can truth and logic be formed to answer relative questions.

* READ - ENJOY – BE FREE *

Dear Editor,

Here is data that you may deem important before going to press.

First Edition – 'The Rose Manuscript' - Copyright 2000 L.A.Dieleman
Renamed and revised 2006 edition – 'The Key to Our Soul Internet'
The complete revised edition as is, was not copyrighted but the
pseudonym 'Stanley Chair' for both editions will remain the same.

On the re-edited material just sent, it was assumed that chapter
heading excerpts would be a curiosity stimulant for the reader to
further explore the chapters' contents. This may seem radical to a
literary status quo that have yet to recognize tradition as 'an overripe
apple' that fell from a tree of outdated knowledge. It would be
gratifying to have us remain in character though and have it printed
exactly as typed.

Poems – 'Rotate with Eight' - Copyright 1996 L.A.Dieleman – the
plus two were added later for total of ten poems. Pseudonym - 'Larry
A'dee'
Note: - The 9th and 10th poems did not come under the '96 copyright.

For all future correspondence between us, please use the following.
– Stanley Chair - P.O. Box 888224 - Grand Rapids, MI - 49588- 8224
USA. This precaution is taken for various security measures but if
for some reason that you must have a quick response, then please
phone my Granddaughter for I have a bad hearing problem and she
will contact me, then call back as soon as possible. Leave your name
and office number to be reached. She designed the cover for the
manuscript but if it can be improved in some way, suggestions too
will be welcomed.

My granddaughter' name is Sarah Dieleman and her cell phone number is 516-1955. Preferably, no E-mail should be used between you because the least exposure before printing would be considered best.

Sincerely,

THE MISSED TARGET

(Because mental harm may not be visible or results immediately known, it is commonly ignored)

Much has been said by a myriad of writers and supposed experts stressing solutions to a variety of the social ills that plaque humankind. Why is it that after their ideas are implemented, our earthly problems still exist and we keep repeating the same errors? We have strived for peace and understanding among ourselves for untold centuries but to no avail. On top of that, life becomes more complex with each generation. With great strides in science and technology, why are we still fighting one another and running around in bewilderment searching for social answers? While many professions progress rapidly, others remain static and stagnate in their fields of endeavor. The latter are pedant and rarely question given data or are reluctant to seek alternatives. They encompass only what was programmed into their memory bank on the brain's left hemisphere while important data and help from the other hemisphere is sadly neglected. If these muscles are not exercised, they too will become weak and dysfunctional like any other body part that is not used. It then becomes difficult to grasp the whole picture that must be conveyed for a logical conclusion. This reflects a large part of our social attitudes where very little thought is given to 'what's behind the paint' as it were, and if relativity is not practiced we are apt to be like a dog chasing its own tail. Though good memory is a big asset, without the clues and assist from our ' total headset ' logic may be limited to ' punch card data ' of a knowledge that already could be obsolete.

Many times, people are put in jail for physical abuse that may heal in a short time, but seldom is the same justice applied to mental abuse that can cripple someone psychologically for life. Because mental harm may not be visible or results immediately known, it's commonly ignored.

We are often concerned with environmental pollution that affects our physical health, but give far little thought to the dangers of mental pollution that can rob us of enjoying a successful and fulfilling life. Questionable and corrupted thought is often a far greater threat to our well being because it contributes to a wider scope of negative feedback. Promoting mind control fear is the evilest of sins! Fear stifles freedom of logical thinking and can result in neurotic problems that later could involve the whole gamut of our social activity with no guarantee of it ending up being mildly damaging or explosively detrimental. In either case, the negative impact becomes a social problem that eventually has to be dealt with.

Too often we rely on the contaminated thoughts of others and then become a stereotype of their views, while a perfectly good thinking device on the top of our neck remains dormant. Insecurity is often a major factor, for fear of being different or not having matured enough to be confident in thinking for self. We are then apt to be vulnerable to such things as innuendo, rhetoric, propaganda, traditional ideology, etc.

The strongest barrier to free thinking and enlightenment is by far that of rigid ideological thought. Most were raised in fear of being damned and doomed unless certain concepts were followed. This ploy puts a 'straight jacket ' on our freedom of thought and it remains a mind control tool of many religions today. When these irrational ideas are researched, however, it boils down to words of some extinct author whose concepts had no valid proof, other than the hearsay of someone else's imaginary illusions. Research was seldom sought for past information was scarce and unreliable, plus logic of both brain hemispheres had not yet matured.

When certain concepts were adopted by government leaders, they were then forced on the masses who feared persecution if they were out of step with their rulers. These concepts were then generally followed by succeeding generations and became our traditional belief systems.

By clinging dogmatically to ignorance inherited from forebears we have stereotyped the way most of our societies are governed today.

Mind pollution plays on fear, prejudice and false pride in ideologies and eventually turns to hate against any opposing thoughts and is a root cause of most human suffering, past and present including wars. Free will is meaningless and cannot be manifested successfully until we are aware of and respect factors other than our own. All universal action relates to the law of cause and effect and if we fail to realize this, our present life on earth may very well become a wasted adventure. Many religions try to sanctify their myths and fantasies as replacements for civil progress and scientific logic. The practice and patience of science in researching the intricacies of nature and its related life has given us far greater knowledge of our environment and statistical data in physics than any other medium. If all of nature is the handiwork of God and science discovers more facts concerning creation; then we must conclude that science earns the status of a Divine undertaking and to disagree with that would be hypocritical.

From becoming victims of ignorant thought or the tutors thereof, we should always seek relative answers to what, where, when, who, why, etc. If the results are still not clear, we should research the subject when time permits. Egos delude us into assuming that we are civilized people. With all of the bias, prejudice and hate that ideologies are guilty of, this most certainly cannot be the case. To avoid future traumas in our lives, it would be wise to rearrange priorities and work on changing various attitudes also. It is far more important to find the keys on HOW we should think in a relative way rather then blindly accept the dogma of others on WHAT they want us to think. We can forgive illiterate forbears who lived in fear of a mythical hell and brainwashed into accepting unproven myths and fantasies. However, we must wonder why these fanatical beliefs still continue in a more educated world?

Why is our brain's right hemisphere so little used today with all the knowledge that is now available? Is religion's hypothetical tool 'faith' the culprit of creating illusionary security and erecting a barrier between brain hemispheres and suppressing desire for more knowledge? Faith makes it easy for the lethargic mind to drop the work of finding answers and forming own opinions. Personal evaluation is not a freedom that is favorably looked upon by a religious status quo of preconceived ideas. When religious doctrine is questioned, the usual response is not rational reasoning but often a threat of the warm variety.

Occasionally, there are apt to be few religious minds that jump over the faith wall temporarily and come up with some pretty good stuff. But, when analyzed by the fear and fantasy side; it's burned and buried in like manner as sanity is treated. If truthful data is a survival requisite of our predicted new age to come, would western religions then be doomed?

If others are allowed to pollute our thinking, we will then become steppingstones for them to wipe their feet on and they in turn are apt to control the destiny of our birthright. Dictatorial people whether one or many are nothing more than predators, whose greed, vanity and lust for power precedes all else. We will know them by their pollution of the environment, ravaging the earth's resources and subduing the human resources as well. Adhering to the law of the jungle they have no more conscience than that of a wild beast.

There is a lack of respect for others who contributed to their wealth and fought the wars that preserved their lifestyles; by shipping work to other countries and allowing the real patriots to loose their possessions that they worked so hard to get. These polluted minds show no concern for the welfare of those below their status and consider them expendable human equations. They influence the passage of corrupted laws to their advantage making them a legal farce that has very little import on the true meaning of justice. It appears that pollution has many facets.

ATTITUDE

(Taking one step forward scientifically and two steps backward socially, the only dance step we know?)

When faced with the task of solving dilemmas, our society continues to reach into ideological 'grab bags' for solutions that ultimately become duds. A noted weakness is the variety of 'grab bags' available and by choosing one over another creates friction and more problems to solve. A much better purpose would be served if these 'bags' were draped over a user's head and the contents never revealed. We receive an education to encourage intelligence and then use past concepts for solving today's problems, rather then utilizing available data as compensating tools of perception.

Ancient opinions of good and evil are parroted without analytical thought or research and it seldom enters programmed minds that these are merely personal evaluations on how it affects certain people. What may be good for one can be counterproductive to another and considered evil. The whole concept of good and evil is arbitrary and variable.

What is happening to us? Aren't we supposed to be an enlightened species with a civilization to match? Is one step forward scientifically and two backward socially, the only 'dance step' we know? Whatever alibis are used, one dominant factor stands out; it is traditional attitudes that stifle us from thinking for ourselves. Because of this, we allow tainted professionalism to control a portion of our lives and complain when things go wrong. For fear of change we tend to ignore alternatives and enslave ourselves to the status quo.

Much of the hearsay, rhetoric, old wives tales, etc. that was handed down to us, are assumed to be correct with no logical or credible proof thereof. Many other methods used are never challenged, even though our intuition tells us there is something amiss. To seek alternatives may mean change and civilization has fought it until they were overwhelmed.

Our complacency in biased beliefs often sanctions temporal authority and control to those least qualified for the job. Even when mistakes are obvious, the ego of programmed minds will alibi and continue to support and compound their errors of choice as if no 'delete key' ever existed.

In search of security we seek the illusionary perfection of rigid concepts that resists required flexibility for progressive thinking. When this happens the ego 'shuts the door' on rational reason and we become prisoners of our idiosyncrasies.

To be totally honest, we must question present beliefs. If our parents were of different religious or political concepts, would we also believe in them? The odds are favorable in that direction and by so doing, have we yet to think for our self? Children are expected to copy family attitudes but as adults, shouldn't we become more tolerant of diverse thought and respect the variables in our society?

Life is much like a wheel that is supported by five spokes, all of which must be balanced for the wheel to run smoothly. Let's say ---

The first spoke is INFORMATION that is mind programmed.

The second spoke is BELIEF in the data that is assumed to be correct.

The third spoke is EMOTION, where ego supports our belief.

The fourth spoke is ATTITUDE that becomes top opinion authority.

The fifth spoke is DECISION in action, concluding all is in balance.

The RESULT reflects the sum total of balance in all of the spokes. When the outcome doesn't give the desired effect, however, most of us will go back to the last spoke and hope a change there will solve the problem. This usually fails miserably for other spokes then become out of balance. We literally ignore the ingredients in the rest of the recipe that 'botched the batch.' If spoke one is out of balance and is ignored; trying to compensate with adjustments of others down the line, has little chance of success. This is evidenced in the Arab, Israeli crisis, as it is with most other worldwide disturbances.

The majority of imbalances begin with spoke One. Adhering to data of organized belief systems that seek a common denominator of power and control will have a very negative impact on ensuing efforts. When such systems dominate, they inhibit potential growth of thought because most become outdated object referrals and dependency on them is like a drug to the mind. The ego stands guard over all of our illusionary securities with clenched fists, as it were, and if challenged, no amount of logical persuasion is apt to change its position.

In his book, "Ageless Body, Timeless Mind " Deepak Chopra states that two percent of American people think, three percent think they think and the rest of them would rather die than think. The majority appears to be content going through life functioning from memory and copying what others think and do. This will adhere closely to brain hemisphere concepts outlined in the previous "Missed Target" chapter.

Though Chopra's presumption may have seemed quite true a decade ago; there is however, a beacon in our future. Advanced computers used by younger generations and those that follow, gives them more hands on capability of researching various things that are questionable. This will employ the use of both brain hemispheres more frequently and in recent tests there was a dramatic improvement in relative thinking abilities.

We can perceive that sound thinkers will be a majority in the future after most adult generations have passed on, taking with them traditional prejudices and fantasies that burdened humanity for countless centuries. This improved condition is essential for the earth's new Aquarian Age to function properly. The life stage set before us may not be to our liking at present, but it is all part of evolutionary lessons that must he gained in our time. If for any reason we suspect our attitude of becoming too bias in a negative way, it might be wise to nudge the ego aside temporarily and readjust our wheel of life starting with the first spoke.

To review our humility status from time to time is always a good idea.

This often produces a surprised confession, "I didn't know that"?

It is our choice to go through life as mere followers and lackluster observers or 'tough it out' and climb to a higher plane of awareness for which our life purpose was intended. To start 'the ball rolling' the three important R's, must be observed and that is to read, research and refine. No book or idea can 'stand alone' for they are only the work of human perception that is prone to error much of the time.

Trying to erase all negativity that accumulated in a mind's computer over the years is quite an impossibility for this would signify reaching a goal of perfection and we are not logically at that stage of advancement in this lifetime. Let us not be ashamed of unknowingly eating a couple of "bad apples" at one time or another, for these are comparative lessons designed for our progress.

A humble desire for truth will eventually be gratified by knowledge and wisdom that will free us to think individually and be our self.

When this is accomplished we will no longer be fooled by charlatans or become the tools for predators who are waiting to 'in the wings' to devour us. We will soon realize that darkness is the absence of light in the esoteric sense, so negativity is only temporary and will disappear when exposed to light. Light is positive and a growth factor. Consider this when we are comparing knowledge to light and vice versa. This is very important for how flexible our attitude is, will determine the direction in which we are heading.

KNOWLEDGE

(Soon after being introduced, new knowledge is apt to be on the 'skids' of already becoming obsolete)

The key of using knowledge to solve problems depends on our ability to cope with the following fact. With the exception of math and proven science, knowledge is a form of hearsay or drawn conclusions that is subject to revision and change. Soon after being introduced, much of knowledge is already in the process of becoming obsolete. When this is fully understood, it can no longer be treated as absolute or pristine. These attributes belong to what some call the Divine Mind and logically speaking, only this First Cause can know Self.

Superficial data without proof or logic remains illusionary and when accepted emotionally for any reason, it becomes dogmatic in nature and shuns the rationale of other views or new information. This reaction is then considered blind belief.

To the other extreme, when certain portions of knowledge appear weak or unfounded, the whole is also likely to be rejected. The reason for this is that anything less than perfection is usually repugnant to a conditioned or programmed mind. Total rejection, however, may ignore certain aspects of information that are true and useful; whereas the rest of it may be quite tolerable for the time being or discarded by choice. The point is, to exercise our logic and remain flexible enough to accept data that appears to have justifiable truths. If necessary we will then be able to comfortably alter our concepts accordingly. To do less, is denying self the growth of mind and character.

The ego often rejects logic to protect the illusionary security to our comfort zones. Another traditional habit is that of relying on the many documented references to boost credibility. This is a numbers game to shore up human insecurity and is common in many fields of endeavor, professional or otherwise. It gives the impression that we are smarter than we actually are or presents a phony façade of respectability.

The weakness of this procedure shows up in time spans where numerous things that were considered correct, was later found to be dangerous or detrimental. Miscalculations in the medical and engineering fields are prime examples that the majority of opinions must always be open for challenge or debate. Most concepts are copied opinions of someone else and seldom encompass pure personal logic or in depth research. It then comes as no surprise that superstitions, tradition, rhetoric and old wives tales have at times also influenced popular opinions.

Some literary works are produced that cater to the understanding level of specific groups such as professionals and this would naturally entail required references. Other than that, unless we are in the teaching field, it's best to keep references to a minimum, for if properly presented the logic is immediately recognized by knowledgeable readers. Too many references in a work gives an impression that the author seeks support from others because of weak content or to project an illusion of being well informed. If any serious material can't stand alone on the strength of reason then it shouldn't be presented. To prevent a mental lockup, we must view most reported hearsay as temporal for it's based only on the knowledge that is available at the time of conception. We should visualize and treat the use of data as a mental TOOL and shy away from a temptation of regarding it as rigid fact. A general misconception with many is that having quick memory recall designates intelligence. Being able to recognize a tool and its use is but a small portion of intelligent design. Of greater importance is our capacity to analyze and use the tool correctly to attain positive results. When tools become more efficient, it is advantageous to use the most refined model. Just as machinery is improved or replaced with state of the art units, knowledge must be treated in like manner and as it grows, progression and change are inevitable. Lack of awareness for reading this 'blue print' of evolution correctly may bring about a host of problems that we must face later.

Over emphasis on individualism will put a 'damper' on our social growth, forgetting that we are all but a small part of the whole. Avid personal concern is the forerunner of avarice that pushes aside public justice, respect for the environment and a loss of psychic sensitivity. Should the basic elements of our coexistence continue to be ignored, we shall destroy the necessities for survival of future generations.

Using the tool of knowledge as its foundation, the purpose of philosophy is to reach the closest factual conclusion of any theme in the most rational manner by logic deduction. Of course, the reliability of any truism is reflected by the quality of data received and the capacity of a mental level to analyze it correctly. Should any conclusion become a concept, it must be treated as only temporal for consistency is always relative to workable time spans, which may be of short or long durations. Protecting its value, philosophy must adhere to natural law and always remain flexible enough to accept any new and justifiable information. It is also necessary for egos to remain relatively humble and strong enough to steer clear of adamant issues.

RELATIVITY

(If relativity hasn't become part of our deductive reasoning, we are still 'spinning our wheels in low gear' as it were)

Nothing under the sun is entirely positive or negative and if it were possible, we wouldn't be aware of it. Both must function together in some degree before either can manifest itself. Generally speaking, to have a greater realization of anything we must have comparative values surrounding it, be it substance, dimension or color. Also, from a logical standpoint we need evil to tell us what is good and the largest part of this awareness operates on personal observations and balances. Premises are formed through observation or hearsay and conclusion is usually reached by an expression of assumed logic. Whether personal or not, all logic has a considered value and this is determined by the quantity and quality of evidence that supports the premise. How credible is personal logic if it involves a fantasy that the moon is made of green cheese? If scales of equality tip heavily to one side we can reasonably presume what the end result should be. Conversely, if little or no information is there to justify the premise, it must be classified as unsound until multiple factors prove otherwise.

All this has to do with comparative thinking and if relativity hasn't become a part of deductive thought, then our 'wheels are still spinning in low gear' as it were. Without this relative key we become like parrots squawking rhetoric and hearsay with little realization of what it's all about. During our schooled education we were inclined to accept as factual all that was taught us. It was fine with the A B C's and certain sciences but most of past societies were delinquent in researching events of historical significance and dealing truthfully with human equations. Teachers were victims of this systematic stigma and are not to blame for what was then taught as presumed truths. Dogma of the earlier days was injected into our educational systems and this became traditional mindset for generations to come.

Majority concepts came from prejudiced and biased opinions in an era that was short on syllogistic reasoning and ignored the value of relative deduction. Many centuries had passed before some enlightened authors braved the indignation of the status quo by researching more accurate accounts of historical events and exposing their true significance. But, even after apparent proof by the best of research, there appears no rush to correct textbooks or change traditional teaching habits, per se.

We might ask, "So, what's the big deal"?

To whit – By taking pride in this country's accomplishments while we tend to ignore deceptions of honesty and integrity on the down side is corrupting our political system. Where the 'thread of apathy is woven into the fabric of our national character, it triggers irresponsibility and cover-ups that spreads throughout the society like wildfire. This malady stretches across the whole spectrum of national thought, thus creating attitudes of bigotry in economics, religion, politics, etc. Excluding the sciences, our society is still engrossed in images and symbols. Perfect imagery of our democracy must be preserved at all cost and patriotism becomes a hypocritical emblem of 'all for one and one for all.'

We condemn the Japanese for not telling their people the truth about Pearl Harbor; but are too ashamed to admit the fact of our choosing a murderer for President in 1840 when Wm. H. Harrison was elected on the slogan, 'Tippecanoe and Tyler too'. As a general, Harrison decided that killing Indians would give him the popularity that he sought, for most white people in those days not only feared the native race but also wanted the land they occupied. Harrison took advantage of an Indian spiritual gathering at Tippecanoe and on the premise that it was an Indian uprising he massacred hundreds of men, women, and children. A hunger for sensationalism by newspapers escalated Harrison to a hero status. This action was never truthfully related or officially rescinded.

Later in the century, General George Custer too, had aspirations of becoming President. He married a judge's daughter for the purpose of social acceptance and sought to follow the success formula of Harrison. Only this time, miscalculation caught his troops in a vulnerable position and he and all his men were wiped out. The prejudiced press and biased historians of that era and even some today still make Custer a martyred hero which influenced the hatred toward Indians for generations to come.

Many more infamous deeds were committed over the years by Americans, both here and abroad. The point is, that to regain national respect we must resort to honesty and stop glorifying wars and killing for invested interests. Why are we exposing young minds to killing cartoons on TV when they are scarcely out of diapers? Where are mass killing ideas among students coming from? We know but tend to ignore any problem that isn't close to us.

Traditional teaching methods are still practiced where discipline is a priority above student respect. This promotes many problems we have with students today; something that could be corrected but the status quo remains apathetic to change. Instead of being treated as equal souls in a learning process, they are being talked down to; all this comes through like a 'ton of bricks'. Should the student be a highly advanced soul, such treatment would be even more difficult to accept. This is pertinent to the fact that many troublemakers have brilliant minds and resent what they witness. The rebellious will use disruptive tactics as compensation for their plight or call attention to inequities. Insensitivity of counter egos refuses to recognize the situation and only see the acts as incorrigible disobedience.

At present, these youths have yet to realize, as it is with many of us, that they are here to observe and like everyone else learn tolerance in so doing. To be successful it must be accomplished through the bonding of teacher and students in the lower grades.

This is where the most experienced and highest paid teachers should be. We should give our public teachers the best of our support for they work under handicapped conditions that very few of us realize. They must handle not only racial differences but also those in language; all of this besides trying to overcome ignorance fantasies that were taught many students by earlier religious affiliations. Teachers were not given the necessary preparation to handle all the abstract traditions they now face.

Evolutionary progress in social matters is very slow at times but then again, revolutionary action often produces negative side effects for a long time after. It should be realized that the pendulum of life returns from extremes in like manner. Positive growth is best accomplished by tolerant attitudes and we must not be overly concerned of finding perfect answers because there are none; only better ones. Ours is a very complex society with many choices of endeavor but ignoring relative factors can jeopardize chances to progress. In other words, to turn a corner in the right direction we must recognize the validity of other views and learn to compensate. Relativity is a natural condition of universal comparisons.

What Albert Einstein proved with relativity in a materialistic sense is also applicable to other aspects of our existence. Unless, our thinking is done in a relative manner we will become easy victims to all sorts of innuendo and propaganda. There is still a resistance by people toward the evolutionary principles of science and for no rational reason other than some instilled religious concepts and the immaturity to think for themselves.

Science studies nature's laws and the more facts that are uncovered, brings us nearer to understanding our beautiful universe. From this we can better perceive our purpose in this dimension. While studying short life cycles under a microscope we perceive how living organisms mutate and evolve; this among other things supports the theory of evolution and gives us assurance of a natural law not based on mythical fantasy.

Throughout history discoveries made by science have disturbed those who relied on superstitious beliefs to control ignorant masses. Everyone is aware that the universe had to be created from something and could not be made from nothing but for some ancient writers to believe the world was flat and the center of the universe, showed our ignorance of scientific knowledge back then. This and a theoretical time table put on the origin of our universe makes for another no-brainer. Evolution as demonstrated in nature is a key factor to all that is, even to including our existence. From the knowledge gathered of science we were able to invent the many things we now enjoy and take for granted. A 'wave' religion likes to make against evolution centers on our soul body. To try and guess the precise time a soul is made or how it enters the body is mere conjecture and if belief is that only the Divine creates souls also, then what's the point? Are we creating more human myth and fantasy? To make evolution more understandable, we must become aware of its action. It should be realized that ENERGY is never lost; but changes form and that all things have Positive and Negative Polarities.

The logical conclusion in science is that various elements under certain conditions will produce certain effects in proven laboratory tests and can also apply to the way the universe was created. The phrase, as above so below, reminds us that the earth is a microcosm of a macrocosm.

1. - As the prime element HYDROGEN was condensed, an intense heat developed and from its burning collapse, HELIUM was formed.
2. - When HELIUM went through this same process, CARBON was made.
3. - As CARBON cooled its gases produced vapors that formed WATER.
4. - Impact of the huge combustions created Sunlight, Heat and Radiation that raised CARBON vibrations to the complex molecular levels of MATTER.
5. - MATTER began absorbing MATTER until PLANTS were formed. .
6. - PLANTS then released OXYGEN necessary for ANIMAL life.
7. - First FISH followed by other LIFE, evolved, mutated and adapted to their environment.
8. - As vibration levels of ANIMAL life became higher, HUMANOID bodies began to evolve and progressed to their present state.
9. - SOULS created in the Spiritual World and endowed with Free Will then entered these BODIES for experiences on this Planet.

How does the transition from soul into body than become a living
soul? Ideas vary on this but the most logical conclusion is that transition
takes place after birth when external air bearing NOUS and soul enters the lungs to make the cycle complete.

As all beliefs are temporal, and to relegate them to memory as if perfect would be counter-productive. Though change is ever universal we still drift to a status quo concept of some kind. By opening the door to a higher awareness, it would give us the stability to deal with change as it becomes necessary.

If science admitted there was a God without empirical proof thereof, they would then lose their value as a research institution. On the other hand, if atheism rejects religious gods, their reason is valid but if stated that there is no entity source of power responsible for creation without positive proof, this then weakens their concept, as well.

So far, this leaves only one rational view to consider; who or what is responsible for the cosmic creation and this is a moot question? Cause and effect appears to be the only certainly that it is a dominant law of the universe and as such, it is the base for a realization that other laws must follow. With more overwhelming evidence popping up every year, it becomes increasingly difficult to ignore reincarnation which is based on this universal law also.

Learning to compensate different opinions with tolerance is the best way to begin respect and love of others and this we need to do. Being born into this finite world, the realities and protection of it as our home should be our main concern; not some hypothetical human myth invented for the purpose of power and control. Can anyone adhering to a Holy Book honesty believe that an all knowing Creator would put us in a position where we didn't have the power to correct our mistakes now or at some other time in the future? Would this not mean that our God or powers that be goofed up on creation? Where then would be a sane reason to worship the deity or power that didn't have it all together?

It is human nature for us to try and prove our intelligence or perhaps that of ignorance but whatever is manifested it is still a natural right to progress at our own level of awareness. If we have no tolerance and love left for others then our own progress is in question.

That which is beneficial to our mental security at a given time should be considered a plus. It must not in any way though, be detrimental to others and the environment or the purpose becomes a negative factor. Not everyone has the same level of awareness and all must be given a chance to grow.

To exercise free will, free thought must be a constant companion; for personal progress can only function through individual initiative. If fearful to think for ourselves, we shall remain in darkness, a prisoner of our insecurity.

Fear becomes a paradox to many of us for we fear the truth that in turn could free us from our fears. Strange creatures are we who feel lost without our insecurity. However, the inner light is always there and will patiently wait for us to discover it.

FINDING OURSELVES

(It doesn't take a 'wet mop' in the face to figure out that apathy and procrastination are the by products of ignorance)

There is an inward desire to know more about self and our purpose in life but we are lost on where to begin. To fill the need of additional security to our comfort zones, many of us have succumbed to a variety of answers; illusionary, traditional or otherwise.

Proof of anything relating to the abstract is usually hard to define and some practitioners in the field of psychology have attempted to aid us by using a simple formula. They expound a philosophy of knowing our capabilities with a strong emphasis on positive thinking. This may be helpful in many ways but counter productive in others. More than positive awareness is involved here because it's the understanding of self from an operational point of view that's significantly more important.

It's only natural in wanting to function in the best possible manner, but when positive thinking is used as a panacea for most of our actions, any overkill that is used is apt to create future problems. Daily affairs might be managed quite well at times by projecting a positive outlook, but when it tends to ignore or cover up adverse factors, it fractures or delays an overall positive effect. The negative aspects will show up later, in one form or another, until we can appropriately deal with them.

All have been guilty of repeating a phrase without much thought, because of its 'pleasant ring'. Thus, it is with 'positive thinking' a term that is so often used as a crutch to elude responsibility. It is regularly injected into debate when some weakness is discovered.

It may go something like this, "Hey let's forget it, think positively, nothings perfect and we are a lot better off than so and so."

This thought makes about as much sense as two fellows fishing on a lake and one calls the others attention to a hole in the bottom of the boat.

The reply is, "Relax, buddy, don't worry, we're in better shape than that guy over yonder who has a bigger hole in the bottom of his boat."

So, by the time they figure out why the other guy is suddenly in the water swimming for shore, it's too late to plug the hole in the bottom of their boat because water is already running over the gunwales and they find themselves rapidly sinking. It doesn't take a 'wet mop' in the face to realize that apathy and procrastination are by products of ignorance.

Ducking our head in the sand when things are not to our liking accomplishes only temporary respite from the surrounding world of reality. The whole gamut of life, from early cognizance until transition, is an experience of comparisons and from these we must also learn to compensate. Unless, presented lessons are honestly embraced, we are forfeiting meaningful portions of our lives. For example, living under a shield of positive illusions, can never bring the satisfaction or elation that comes from solving and correcting problems during negative situations.

Norman Vincent Peale once stated, "thank God for problems". He was aware that we couldn't mature mentally and progress without them.

Along with the process of aging, the more we become creatures of habit and resistant to change. Thus, the axiom 'that you can't teach an old dog new tricks.' This need not be so, however, for our reluctance to learn is more of an attitude than an age factor. To progress in anything, a higher level of awareness is achieved and with this, change is inevitable.

In Maxwell Maltz's book, 'Magic Power of Self Image Psychology' he uniquely reasoned that the majority of us are prodded to change by Divine discontent. We can surmise that he was trying to impress the religiously inclined people whose minds are most resistant to change because of Divine reliance and a fear of any change to their status quo. Productive change is usually thwarted by those traditionally influenced.

Often the search for identity and purpose in life is sidetracked and our main objective becomes material gain.

More than anything else, excessive materialism will retard our psychic growth because greed runs counter to our soul contract, as it were. We must realize that such action actually trades off the positive aspect of attaining a higher awareness of life for a false sense of security.

The most common obstacle to finding ourselves and fulfilling our potential is fear. Fear of committing an error may seem insignificant but it is an overriding hindrance to positive thinking. Most of us still cling to a two faceted belief of right and wrong and a mistake would seemingly apply to the wrong side and create subtle feelings of guilt. We fear the judgment of peers who may think less of us if our errors were exposed. It is necessary to rationalize fears and recognize them for what they are, so our path ahead may be cleared for us to think and act freely.

Though perfection may be a worthwhile goal, we must come to grip with the fact that it cannot be an actuality in this world's dimension. If we expect perfection of self, there will be a constant struggle with our ego and if we demand it of others, strife is sure to follow.

All of nature functions under the law of cause and effect. As such, any action taken will ultimately determine a judgment that we cannot escape. And if we see only black and white with no shades of gray in between, then its a no win contest between our egos and reality.

What we think, say or do, so long as it bears an honest trademark, is nothing to be ashamed of. Even when in error, if it's right for us at the moment and not detrimental in any way to others; then there is no sane reason why guilt should enter into our learning process. Be rest assured that more refined data will be made available when we are duly prepared to handle it. To quote an axiom, 'When the student is ready, the master will appear.' The main ingredient of progressive action is change and it may become necessary to embrace it in many ways.

The discipline in change is apt to include not only attitudes but our concepts and ways of living, as well.

When dealing in comparisons, we can never hold ourselves above someone else because of some special attribute or gift that was bestowed upon us. Those not at the high level in something as another person, can have a far greater talent in a different field that has yet to develop into a visible reality. As more wisdom is acquired, it will be realized how little we actually know. Assuming that sand was a measure of wisdom and a few more grains were held in our hand than that of someone else. What then would be the reason to feel superior when a surrounding beach with tons of sand is still waiting to be claimed?

By discarding less meaningful things, a keener perception of truth will usually follow. By comparison, it would be like observing the world through our picture window to that of surveying the beautiful panoramic view of it from a mountaintop. From the larger vision, we can absorb the majestic feeling of creation and sense being an integral part of all that is.

As knowledge of self grows, it opens the door to a higher awareness of life and our purpose is clarified. That which is revealed to us from our inner self can be very helpful in numerous ways. It produces an edge to everyday decisions and final conclusions will come from the coordinated response from both our objective and subjective senses. Thus, both brain hemispheres will be working together and become the basic key for the manifestation of wisdom.

Certain talents or inner desires should not be discarded for they may be the best course to follow. We must not be discouraged by temporary set backs as they may be necessary lessons to try other means. Some worthwhile goals may take longer because there are always 'rivers to cross' but by remaining focused and through continued effort, we can literally 'build bridges' to meet the other end.

There is also much knowledge of self to be gained through the eyes of others, for in us they see, what our egos don't want portrayed. In retrospect, clues from these encounters can present a more accurate picture of knowing ourselves.

As our awareness becomes more acute and we sense the source of cosmic love that resides within, then a wordless communication of peace and harmony can be manifested among those that we meet. When these higher vibrations are forthcoming, a deeper love of life is experienced and no longer would we render hate nor harm unto another. We can then be ourselves and not copious of others, unless of course, we would rather desire to act like parrots or clones.

Using the gift of mind as best we can, is the only requirement that is needed to begin progressive thinking and a key to wisdom is contingent on the quality sessions we have with our soul internet.

Patience and tolerance must be practiced continually for it is not an easy attribute to maintain. As mother earth was not created in a day nor will she die in like manner. We don't know precisely the timetable that is bestowed upon another human; from being born to transition; nor all the acts and experiences that he or she will have during their lifetime. We cannot literally live in another's shoes and at times we must give them room for personal experiences and decisions so that they can find themselves in a natural way. A few years ago, the thought of a young adult speeding down a steep inclined handrail on a skate board would have brought the screams of mothers hollering, "Stop, or you will surely kill yourself." .

The kids now join organized contests in which they receive medals for their dangerous sport. Then with mom's approval these now hang on the fireplace mantle. It is all about conquering our fears and challenging tradition to change. People will try to find themselves in various ways.

QUEST FOR TRUTH

(Complete truth per se, is unfathomable, it just is and nothing can be added or deducted from it by human thought)

If the consensus is that we're not here by mistake, than a logical conclusion is that our lives are a learning experience of coping with a truth when it's revealed to us, in this beautiful dimension. The degree of truth realized depends largely on our ability to analyze its accuracy by complete reasoning of our objective, subjective and deductive faculties.

For the soul to progress in the best possible way, the shroud of fear and ignorance that is passed on to us in the form of preconceived ideas must be replaced with the most positive aspects of truth at hand. Only a higher First Cause per se, can know the absolute of anything.

We must remember too while doing research that no idea or book can 'stand alone' either. The range and depth of truth is determined by testing its consistency. For example, we know the truth in mathematics by continual accuracy of its results and as this proof becomes evident, it then takes on the status of a law. That which is not consistent in proof, is weak in content or degree of truth and unless this is clearly understood there is little chance of us evolving along with the perception of truth. Certain formulas are applied to math to achieve accurate results but with most other information that we receive, sane reasoning must be used to obtain suitable answers. If our memory can't give us the answers, than the data must be researched. How we re-act to any given idea depends on our reasoning power and the capability to think for ourselves. Most solutions are formed from data or hearsay that is stored in our memory bank and how much analytical thinking has been applied to them is a moot question. The human brain is much like a computer and since birth it has been the recipient of continual programming; most of which is accepted without empirical proof.

The longer data is stored in memory, it becomes hardcore and is more difficult to correct or erase.

For centuries our society has influenced the human mind to accept but two options, black and white with no shades of gray in between. Prominently promulgated were the rigid opposites of right or wrong, friend or foe, love or hate, etc. A glorified option still overused today is that of win or lose. It appears that ties are actually detested and must be played off to decide a winner. Though we pay lip service to equality, there seems little satisfaction derived from being equals in our society. It is a sad and archaic condition that persists in sports when we 'red shirt' or 'bench warm' youngsters that denies them equal time and sharing a feeling of oneness with other team members. They graduate as young adults with a lowered self esteem, thrown into a 'dog eat dog world' that society has created and are then pressured to meet challenges of life in a first team fashion. When is our sanity going to put tradition on a shelf and realize that attitudes and growth of minds are far more important than winning scores and promotion of coaches, school officials, etc. With the rash of drug abuse and suicides among our stressed out young people today, it would be wise to question certain academic programs and take a hard look at some status quo 'hang ups' in our business and social world as well. Aspiring to be Number One in sports also carries over into the business world where millions of dollars are spent with no holds barred to secure a top ranking while ignoring the harmful feedback it creates for people in the communities. There seems to be a vital lack of conscience or morals where money is concerned and monopoly laws are skirted to benefit hostile takeovers of smaller businesses.

Many of our social problems are the direct result of our gullibility in placing too much value in preconceived ideas that are lacking in proof or logic. These attitudes usually find us 'painting ourselves into a corner.'

Then when faced eventually with the reality of our error, an illusionary pretext is usually sought by the ego.

Searching for perfection we fall victim of seeking correct answers from those whom we have given temporal authority to guide and control our lives. Implanted fears and superstitions have robbed us of the very important need to think for ourselves. We become afraid to use various tools of available knowledge and attempt to fill this gap with fantasy and hearsay that have little or no proven factors.

The perception of truth should never be limited to one source or a confined group of like thought where nodding accents produce nothing more than transient pleasures of confirming bias convictions. Truth, per se, is unfathomable and just is and we cannot add or deduct from it. Human belief in observation is based on the fragile hypothesis of our experience and intelligence. All dialogs must have an open end for the refinement of added knowledge. As this is practiced, we will gradually progress from the shadow of ignorance into a brighter light of reality and question anything we so desire. This is the souls' birthright and the truth will then be clarified in a manner that conforms to the awareness level of the seeker.

Contrary to the illusion of popular belief, we cannot love with any degree of continuity an abstract being whom we fear, for contradictions of logic such as this cannot exist together. Hence, love of the Divine can only be verified by that shown toward the Creator's finite children and the respect given to all of creation. Humility is a must and it should preclude our awareness of being an integral part of the universe. When this attitude becomes a realization we will then find peace as responsible caretakers of our earthly home, working in harmony with all life therein.

Logic is blending available knowledge with past experience and evaluating it to the highest peak of reason syllogistically.

The duration of logic, however, must be viewed as temporal to coincide with that of evolutionary change. Faith is a positive working tool of confidence in conjunction with truth based on natural law. When the word 'faith' is based on a lesser meaning or use, it has little power and becomes nothing more than a psychological placebo. Faith has no power when it is founded on superstition, fantasy or unqualified hearsay.

To change our way of thinking engenders the same for habits and is not an easy task for an evolutionary process must also take place in our consciousness. Habitual patterns are not quickly altered and ample time must be given for the mind to adjust. If the habit is not positively dealt with, a hiatus is liable to remain and thus, it is not likely to be conquered.

Becoming aware that our beliefs are not pristine as once imagined, a feeling of anger and betrayal ensues. More often then not we will then reject the beliefs entirely and attempt to put them behind us because they did not live up to expectations. Depression can be kept to a minimum, however, once this situation is understood.

As small children we trusted and believed implicitly in our parents and this filled an important need at a crucial time in our lives; but as we became older, it was discovered that Mother wasn't always right nor Dad was the strongest man in town. Yet, we did not reject them because they were not all we imagined them to be.

Take nature, for instance, it has provided us with nourishment and air to physically survive, but even this is not one hundred percent refined for our body's use. In the same vain, that a body eliminates wastes from its physical intake, it should also be duplicated with what is received at the mental level, also. It's folly accepting food for thought completely from hearsay without evaluating it and rejecting its questionable content. When waste is not eliminated regularly from our body it turns toxic and we become ill. Mental constipation works much the same way and will poison the mind.

This would act much like a virus and could involve not only dangers of psychosomatic side effects but also to our physical health as well. Unfortunately, most of us have difficulty finding the delete key on our mind's 'computer keyboard.'

It's quite conceivable that if the mental garbage, to which we now cling, had weight and proportion we would be crushed and buried in total darkness.

An effort of improving our minds is an infinite process of learning new knowledge and refining what is already there. We shouldn't over react to error or imperfections whether our own or that of others, for various actions in life are teaching demonstrations for our benefit and eventual progress.

The sin, as it were, is not so much in the erring but of ignoring its existence and making no attempt to correct or amend it. This weakness is common with alcoholics, for until they recognize and admit to their problem, no specific therapy will have permanent results. This is not just unique with certain people, however, because all of us are vulnerable to varied psychological 'hang ups' during our life spans.

We have two brain hemispheres that control different functions. Among other things, the right side controls intuitiveness and the left objectivity. When imbalances are noticed, we must be careful not to judge, for there may have been weaknesses caused by injury or illness to some portion of these hemispheres. Altruistic people are born with some drawbacks but many have successfully overcome them and became very brilliant contributors to society in certain areas of endeavor.

Most of traditional concepts have been the major cause of today's problems. There can be little social advancement when we are educated on 'what' to think and seldom taught the integral functions of our brain. Emphasis has been on memory of past data with very little attention to analytical thought.

If we rarely used an arm, over a period of time, it would be difficult to hold the weight of a cup of coffee with that limb. Like any muscle, different parts of the brain most be used and exercised or they too, will become dysfunctional; use it or lose it. Traditional thinking has long had a tendency to restrict independent thinking because of its reliance on the memory portion of the brain. Believing in stereotyped concepts handed down without research or logical debate leaves us vulnerable to religious prejudiced views of perfection. While this gives an illusionary sense of security and obscures the need to question, it also produces bigotry and eventual hatred. Its repetition continues to cripple future generations socially for it produces confusion and difficulties trying to correlate the fantasies of yesteryears with realities of the present. With our analytical faculties weakened by disuse we continue to repeat the same mistakes of past generations who were also thus hampered by traditional thought.

When struggling for answers and never taught to think relatively, we often become victims of our own idiosyncrasies or that of others. Using 'an escape hatch' for ignorance we then reach back to the 'old memory track' and try to solve our modern dilemmas with programmed rhetoric, silly clichés and religious myths.

It's also difficult for many of us to determine the truth in many things because of our dependency during childhood that left heavier thinking to others. As this reliance continues into adulthood, it draws us to leaders or groups that presumably fills this need. Concepts of the mentors are then followed blindly for to question them would be alien to already established patterns in our mind.

When we are made to feel guilty by being judged as dirty and evil from the beginning of our supposed arrival on earth, it is difficult to recognize the truth of our being one with the essence of the cosmic or divine. Does anyone really have the authority to judge a soul's purity other than its Maker?

Isn't this factor alone an insult to the Highest Powers that be? Are we the victims of unproven negative views and fears invented by a few past writers who desired power and control over us?

We harmonize quite frequently with our soul's vibrations when quite young but this ability declines as we get older and begin to adapt to what others want us to think. The cosmic or divine never abandons us for this essence always remains within. We are lost souls only when contact with it is temporarily lost. Logically speaking we cannot lose that which is spiritually inherited from an eternal source.

We continually seek illumination in human structures, proclaimed holy books and glib hearsay, while ignoring the Divine link within our being. From social influence of home, schools, etc., we were taught to rely on information and the opinion of others. It was and is still a taboo with certain factions to question the esoteric thought of the religious status quo, for such would disrupt their authority and control over us.

Mythical concepts weaken as science grows stronger and gives us more profound insights on creation and our spiritual heritage. As a unit of the Divine, we can become attuned to the gift of light within and receive its sublime data. When this is discovered, no longer need we rely on the prejudiced assumptions of biased concepts. By Divine design we are free thinking entities with free wills to match but it is how these coincide that brings us the most successful results.

The axiom, 'Search for the truth and it will be found' is not to be taken lightly. The Divine kingdom is within and without, and our closest awareness of the truth comes from the soul within. On experiencing this cosmic reality, we will benefit from its source and be able to walk in our own light.

For later chapters

That's all it takes, is a couple of natural disasters to weaken us and they will walk right in and make this one of their possessions.

For the religious to profess a love of God and then condone our preempted wars that allow the killing and maiming of people along with the destruction of beautiful environments is pure hypocrisy and whatever alibis exist they skirt the truth. .

THE ASCENDING EGO

(Generous excuses that are used to shield self are seldom granted to those on whom we pass our judgment)

The word 'ego' harbors various values that contribute to differing philosophies as well. No benefit would be derived from finding fault with any concept of the word, for they all have probable points of merit. It's worthwhile, however, that an attempt be made to remove some tarnish that clings to the name.

A logical consensus denotes that the ego is the awareness of self as being separate and unique in a relative position to all else. It being a manifestation of consciousness the ego adheres to cosmic law and treated as a noun, it becomes a something with purpose and power unto itself. From this standpoint, it must be dual in nature with evidence of positive and negative polarities.

Though much has been written about the ego, most references have been in a derogatory vein. Its negativity has been emphasized to such an extent, that it reflects on the semantics of the word in a shaded manner and the meaning is commonly adopted as such. Negative demonstrations resulting in misuse of this marvelous power, produces a radical backlash that calls for eliminating the effect by killing its source. This type of over re-action has plagued human minds ever since they were invented. To find out why thoughts are thus motivated, the basic mechanics of our reasoning must be analyzed.

Our brain like a computer is programmed through thoughts and experiences. 'Garbage in, garbage out' is an important factor because our ego will protect what has been accepted by the brain's computer, regardless of error in the data. When the content is often repeated it becomes habitual in reason and re-action. The support of thought by physical action gives it strength and when a concept or point of reason is duplicated, the more rigid its status will be.

This eventually crystallizes into a rationale that is incapable of accepting anything outside of its personal scope of thought. If reflection to some similar thought or concept appears, a conditioned reflex will respond to the stimuli. It matters very little what errors may be involved, because reactions will coincide with established patterns in the mind. In these instances, truth would wage a losing battle in its attempt to present itself because of strong emotional barriers that have been erected by the ego. This combination strongly resists anything that doesn't conform to data within our memory bank. This also pertains to many new things that are perceived. Much of it is largely treated as alien and must 'stew in the pot' awhile before it can be rationally accepted. On the positive side, a delay to any new transition may provide us with temporary protection to our comfort zone from a 'hostile takeover' until we can properly handle it. Even the removal of a negative thing before it's adequately replaced by something positive, may create a psychological vacuum. The ensuing mental confusion could result in a trauma that debases morale along with producing an adverse 'chain reaction' effect to our physical health, as well A more effective method is to 'plant the seed' and give a person free reign to their reasoning power and hope for the best to happen.

An impetus for change is determined by the value placed on what is already in the 'cooker.' In most instances, the need to evolve slowly is very significant for the success of any transition. A cue from Mother Nature shows us that most evolutionary processes are seemingly slow but deliberate and with good cause.

It's hard to assess things objectively with a high degree of accuracy. We are burdened not only by the imperfection of our objective senses, but also by errors in information and the limitation of past experiences. Being ever mindful of this will give us the ability to maintain flexibility of thought.

If at times, we find the ego slanting toward the negative, we should 'slip it into our back pocket' for a much needed rest. This could serve a dual purpose, for the action might be a welcome respite for family and friends as well. When our mind becomes focused again on the 'We are' instead of the 'I am' it's safe to assume the 'tilt' had been corrected and our ego's short vacation was beneficial to all.

It's harder to perceive the negative aspects of self than to observe it in others. We seem to expect perfection of others but seek alibis when in error our self. However, the generous excuses that are used to shield ourselves are seldom granted to those on whom we pass our judgment. We tend to evaluate others from a critical viewpoint and then re-act from that determination.

Though fire has power to hurt and destroy, it does not necessitate annihilating its use, for we know that the power is equally important as a useful tool for good. As in fire, control is the key and the ego should be treated in like manner. This is accomplished by discipline factors, our growth in knowledge and an expanding consciousness. To eliminate or stifle the ego would nullify its intended purpose.

It is impossible for any personal experience to be external of the ego. When anything recognizable is absorbed by our mind, then the experience becomes relative to our self in some expression. Reason tells us that the function of a greater awareness sets us apart from the animal kingdom as humanoids. Proper use of ego awareness gives us control of our lives along with the ability to manage and protect. Without the ego, we would be predominantly motivated by animal percepts, (not precepts) and cellular instincts but this does not coincide with behavior patterns we find in humans. The ego may also be a basic ingredient for performance of our free will and with a relativity presence, it is most likely a valuable tool for creativity, as well.

Projecting our initiative and drive for future action may require the ego's projection of correlating past experiences to those of the present.

It is fascinating to watch an awareness of self develop in infants and the very young. Little of the ego's dark side reveals itself during earlier periods of their growth. It's only as they become older that an awareness of the "I" becomes more entrenched and ego control problems begin to surface.

As values and priorities change and fluctuate with age, so too will polarity shifts of the ego become more evident as it plays out dominant roles. Many don't realize that what they are witnessing at a particular moment is but 'one side of the coin.' In most cases, the negative side is more noticeable and this effect then gives a prejudiced slant to the ego's primary function.

As experiences throughout childhood continue, their growth of accepting family and friends into the ego's realm of consciousness is observed. One of the best examples of the ego's progress comes when two people truly fall in love. When this strong emotion happens, each ego allows a portion of self to be integrated into in a common bond with that of another. What then affects one deeply concerns the other as a personal part of that relationship. As a family grows in number, positive ego factors absorb additional love and commitment. These reflections further expand through social affiliation and things compatible with its nature. Some of them may include loyalty or devotion toward a fraternal organization, spiritual practice, community responsibility, patriotism, etc. These then contribute to the development and progression of their awareness in positive and reciprocating ways. As caring and sharing is blended into the ego, the less of its shaded side will show. By becoming attuned to higher cosmic vibrations, an ego's accent is virtually limitless.

Having acquired humility and immersed in the greater light; then through grace the absolution of our karma will automatically be rectified.

On reaching a higher consciousness, we will be free to choose our soul's destiny. Though all cosmic laws are relative and consistent, we tend to be consistent only with our inconsistency of recognizing this fact and living in harmony with it. To know self we must understand the ego for the two are inseparable. Becoming acquainted with all facets of self is most important for the ego's positive ascent.

To judge the ego's negative 'warp' it is usually easier to discern this by unbiased contacts rather than self. There is always the tendency that we may love us a little too much even in the weak areas. It is sad to say, that this 'negative warp' appears most prevalent in the professional fields as if it comes 'attached' to the sheepskins. A vast percentage seem to be obsessed and pedant with what was taught them and they seldom reach beyond the 'cutting edge.' Adjusting to change is difficult for many to accept; that once was has now become obsolete. Too much security and comfort is given to past standards while ignoring ever evolving cosmic change.

INTERPRETATIONS AND TRANSLATIONS

This excludes mathematical equations and natural law for these would present disparate examples

(The little 's' in semantics can make a big 'S' out of anyone who attempts to marry diverse languages)

The further knowledge travels in time, the less chance it has of conveying the exact content of its genesis. Interpretation begins with a personal evaluation of the written material in hand. Not knowing how many times it was copied or altered before being received, we can only ASSUME the degree of accuracy it contains. In ancient times before the printing press, single copies of supposed originals was handed to others for recopy. With so many fingers 'in the pot' the odds are overwhelming that the pristine quality of the script would suffer and lose some intent. To realize this we have only to look at the existence of seven editions of the Holy Bible, printed at various times over the past few centuries. The material were so tainted, they were referred to as the Seven Evil Bibles. Their contents were altered to degrade women, encourage promiscuity, etc. In this case, not only was the accuracy of interpretation questionable but the integrity of the editing as well. It would be difficult to tell how many errors or changes were made in ancient documents before they were completed.

Translation into different tongues becomes even more difficult each time it is repeated. When an attempt is made to combine the semantics of two languages, intrinsic values become blurred or lost completely. Each translation thereafter will increase the chances for further errors

It could be said, that the little 's' in semantics can make a big 'S' out of anyone attempting nuptial relationships between diverse languages.

In recent times, change of meaning is reflected in some phrases that is mostly an item with the younger set. Very few parents of teenagers today would disagree with this statement.

Their talk doesn't necessarily change the value of dictionary data but rather it creates a combination of words and syllables to express various emotions or ideas. Much of it is like a short hand of speech, in which a few words can take the place of several sentences. These new utterances can't be ignored as a contemporary fad either, for they can fast become a cultural vernacular in the present generation and for some to come.

An example of this is when President Carter visited Poland during his term in office. To illustrate a point he used some words in the native tongue that were given to him by his interpreter describing a serious note in his speech and the people began to laugh. Obviously, his interpreter hadn't mingled with the 'home folks' for some time and never realized that the language could take on a plurality of meaning when uttered in certain ways. To say the least, it was very embarrassing to the President and points out the inconsistency of understanding languages of today, let alone those of the past.

Another quick look concerns the dictator, Saddam Hussein, of Iraq. The name Saddam means 'learned one' or 'leader' in Arabic when the accent is put on the second syllable. Most Americans, however, put an emphasize on the first syllable which changes it to mean 'collision' or 'crash.' Then to take the cake, along comes, Daddy Bush, pronouncing Saddam to rhyme with Adam. The meaning of this is a boy who works at fixing and cleaning shoes, which is the dirtiest of insults in some parts of the Arab world. This demonstrates the delicate balance we have with languages and why we should be cautious to believe presented hearsay and especially so, if it steps back in time.

Most languages constantly grow as the new words formulated in technical and professional fields are gradually added to new dictionaries.

Not too many immediate changes can otherwise be expected, however, for majorities are still captive to old customs and traditions.

As past civilizations evolved, their languages progressed also, but not all at the same pace. When people were captured and enslaved for a time, their speech and that of the conquerors would tend to compliment each other. This then fused into a dialect that further became the basis for reformed languages. We see in the origin of older languages that one word can have several definitions from the way they were used or by the intonations of their syllables.

Even in a supposedly enlightened world, dregs of this system are still with us. The notation under the heading of this discourse bears out this fact. We were probably not aware that as the word PRESENT was quickly scanned over, we unconsciously had to do a double take of it before the gist of the sentence became clear. This is because PRESENT has one spelling for three different meanings; gift, time, and show. If we have slight problems with linguistics now, then picture the difficulties translators might have trying to decipher ancient data minus a dictionary of the period in question.

How are we to definitely know the semantics of languages and in what way they were used thousands of years ago? We would have had to live in the same time span of which the material was written, along with being expertly versed in its use and meaning. This is the only way we could be sure of the validity of a translated document. And, since time machines have yet to be invented, we're back to 'square one'. Imagine the impossible task it would be, having an additional burden of translating the intonations of significant grunts and groans to give the work true validity. In many cases, original material or important bits and pieces of it were lost and assumptions used as replacements. We must rationalize what was involved with many interpretations and translations.

Each writer had the opportunity to insert a personal choice of words they believed would be an improvement over the original script. We must admit to the seed of creativity and invention that is in all of us. Temptation of this sort is a writer's disease not easily handled by the ego. Yet, copied contents of an esoteric nature are still revered by most as being pristine and accepted with no questions asked.

The problem becomes even more complex as diction jumps from language to language, for various values in meaning are always lost in the process. This was demonstrated quite clearly on a TV program some years ago. There were four men, each one adept in three languages. Out of earshot to one another, the host told a joke in English to a Frenchmen who also spoke Spanish and he told it to a Spaniard who spoke Italian.

From Italian it was translated to German. When finally translated from German back to English, the original joke had not only lost its humor but the whole premise made no sense at all.

Common sense tells us, that it would be highly illogical to accept literally as pristine, older manuscripts that were translated. Even with all factors expertly examined and presumed justifiable, we can only assume that the material was interpreted and translated correctly.

An important part of analyzing the precision of any performance, whether it is physical or mental, is to question conditions under which the effort was achieved. If this information is NOT available, then the results are from an ASSUMED position. In any case, it should never be accepted as FACTUAL.

Take the completed work of a translator, for example. What is to determine its accuracy if prevailing conditions during time of transcript is not known? Questions might arise as to the working conditions back then. Was the available light sufficient to see clearly? How good was the translator's eyesight? Was a word illegible or missed? Were there errors in a phrase or paragraph?

Was something left out completely because it was considered unimportant by the copier? Then too, what were the translator's qualifications for the task? Was something taken out of context and given an erroneous meaning? Would the abstaining from a second glass of wine after lunch, have made an import on the script's accuracy?

It's incredulous to think that knowledge in rewritten material could be deemed infallible, knowing that the answers to any of these questions and many more cannot be validated. This is especially important where esoteric values influencing a whole way of life is at stake. Living in an illusionary world while ignoring reality may give us temporary comfort but in the long run, are we not sacrificing precious years negating our purpose in life?

Another credibility factor, not to be overlooked, is the inability of anyone to determine anything from a purely objective state. This is true, whether it is an accident taking place or analyzing some past event.

At the scene of accident, for instance, there can be half a dozen witnesses, all with differing accounts of what happened. From this, it becomes apparent that objectivity is influenced to a great extent by our subconscious memories of past experiences. Along with this, a few prejudiced or biased concepts, additionally thrown in, can really clutter up the picture.

While observing an accident, the various aspects of it may have a different emotional impact with each witness. Past impressions in the memory banks would be correlated with the scene at hand. When asked to recall an incident, certain things may stand out in magnitude to some but would be of minor significance to others. The degree of importance is determined by the impact it had on the subconscious mind. A man is apt to be more accurate describing the mechanics of the action involved while a woman would be more inclined to observe the aspects of human appearances, apparel, etc.

This all relates to established patterns of priority established in our subconscious minds. It matters little whether we are observing directly, reading from a book or just thinking; we can never be totally objective to the actuality of an immediate subject at hand. Much of our awareness functions from past pictures in our mind. These personal memories and clinging emotions will then flood our objective awareness and influence the way things are observed and how the final scene is 'painted.' When we attempt to write an objective article, the mere choice of words and phrases used are a biased contribution of our subjective self.

It was a common practice in past centuries, for authors to infer that what they had written was from a spiritually inspired source, or a direct quote from some renowned holy being. The purpose was to give their work a higher degree of credibility and be more acceptable to the reader. Little progress can be foreseen when rigid concepts are built on the brittle hypothesis of interpretation and translation by a singular or group source. For ages, we've heard the constant echoes of hearsay that certain books were written under the spell of the Holy

Spirit. Of course, a lot depends on whose book we're talking about, as many factions profess having spiritually inspired books.

Quite naturally, only one can be right: so, in the name of God and all things sacred, we begin killing each other to prove ours is the only true God.. Incredibly, the side that lops off the most heads is declared the victor and we bow down in humble gratitude to the Lord for giving us the strength to destroy our fellow beings.

There appears to be more concern with the specifics of theology, which is nothing more than a human THEORY of God, while the basis of Divine spirituality and the application thereof, is continually ignored. This is not to say, that any concept is entirely right or wrong for this is reserved as a personal opinion that all are entitled to have.

What is beneficial to our mental security at a given time should be considered a plus. It must not in any way, though, be detrimental to others and the environment or the purpose becomes a negative factor. Not every soul is at the same level of awareness but all are given a chance to grow. To exercise free will, free thought must be our constant companion and all progress remains an individual initiative.

If we are fearful to think for ourselves, then we shall remain in darkness, a prisoner of our insecurity. Fear to many of us becomes a paradox for we fear the truth that in turn could free us from our fears. Strange creatures are we who feel lost without our insecurity. However, the inner light is always there and patiently waits for us to discover it.

CONCEPTS

(Bias is a universal function and manifests in various ways with most all of creation)

Various concepts are not a prime issue here. The most important factor is to discuss attitudes pertaining to concepts and the necessity for compensating them.

The most harmonizing efforts of successful coalitions for peace or otherwise can be traced to tolerance or constraint toward other views. This is not to say that in the process, all points of opposing concepts would be agreeable and accepted into a common denominator, as this would be rare indeed. The fact remains, that regardless of differences, relationships can co-exist when rational attitudes are mutually applied.

Whereas some philosophers push for an unbiased morality, it's quite unlikely that such a goal can be achieved. Even an agreement to such by a large majority could not make it feasible. Numerous breakdowns are apt to follow for the cloak of bias can never be shed since it is impossible for everyone to attain a same level of logic. Bias should not be confused with prejudice, a word often attached to it in a descriptive manner. To be completely unbiased would imply that we had no inclination, direction or preference. We were never meant to be clones and individual needs plus choices

54

may vary. These differences include nutrition, mental security and even to the selection of colors or music that harmonize with personal scales of vibration. Some activists strive to make unbiased attitudes the common denominator for most goals. This is mere fantasy that creates confusion for nothing can grow or be fruitful from such an ideological combination. As covered in the previous chapter, total objectivity is not logically attainable.

The beauty of nature can be appreciated for its myriad of designs, colors and dimensions in the flora and fauna that surrounds us. We cannot ignore the polarities needed for the natural order of propagating the various kinds.

Bias is a universal function and manifests in various ways with most of creation. It is also part of a duality where the positive and negative must act together. Too often, we are urged into overkill by an emotional reaction to what seems a negative aspect of a bias situation.

A picture of some past negative experience is flashed on the screen of our subjective consciousness and reflected to the objective mind that derides the action we perceive. At times it projects feelings of guilt from previous actions that we are trying to rectify but have yet to reconcile. When this happens there is a 'call to arms' by the ego to subdue a certain bias once and for all. This then results in 'over swing of the pendulum' forcing a reaction from the law of cause and effect.

Wise were the sages of old when they encouraged pursuit of the middle way. Had we heeded their advice, our swan dives into those beautiful pools of illusion, would not have turned out to be belly flops into the muddy waters of reality.

The building blocks of bias must be present to form a concept. The determination of positive or negative influences in any biased action is always relative to the applied circumstances. From a position of opposed views, who will judge the content of bias? To compensate them could be a probability if both parties wore the other's 'moccasins' for a while. But, to gain an introspection of another's reality in this way, is a dubious thought for it is too time consuming. We are all much too busy for this kind of foolishness. It's far easier to ignore and walk away from these problems. Of course if pressured, another common alternative is to bash in the other guy's head, making our point more emphatic. It is sad to see that 'might makes right' is becoming the 'in thing' with today's society.

A most deplorable situation to observe, are various religions around the world at war with one another. Has sectarianism become a higher objective than moral obligations of understanding and love?

Are religious leaders corrupting spiritual responsibility of projecting the Divine essence of love by subsidizing dogma and mind control for mundane advantages? A huge recycling effort is in order if these guilty factions wish to regain respect as peaceful proponents of our Creator. Though love and tolerance has been heavily advocated by religion, a great many of their acts have proved otherwise. History proves that once fundamentalists gain political or regional power they become a militant faction and attempt to destroy anything or anyone opposing their view

It's difficult to reconcile concepts of different faiths because the bias slants are ingrained into habitual patterns relating to illusionary securities of their comfort zones. If there is a challenge to any of these securities, our ego raises its might to protect and preserve it. Sensitivity and growth of egos may vary in complexity and is determined by past experiences and/or relationships Degree and amount of friction that is encountered, will give rise to the type of rationale or action pursued. Mentally, we all have security niches, unique unto ourselves. This helps us to function comfortably as an entity. We should also become more aware of these sensitive areas in others and use discretion when communicating with them. In order to foster friendly relationships, we must recognize the safety perimeters that may be involved.

Participants that have reached a higher plateau of consciousness are always more receptive to open ended dialogue. With the majority of people though, any change to their formed concepts or attitudes takes time, for these must be logically analyzed and accepted before any of their adjustments can be made.

Being accustomed to a modern world of instant packaging, we expect speed and quick solutions to our problems also. We are going through an age where computers have reduced numerous time elements.

The complex form of communication on a personal basis is still an art, however, where haste remains its number one enemy.

At times, differences will seem insurmountable, even though we try to compensate for them with words of respect and understanding. In many such cases, our attitude is often the culprit, for words lose their impact when a feeling of being talked down to is felt. If real concern and brotherhood is displayed we may be pleasantly surprised with the results. Such action may help eliminate some prejudiced ideas we have of others and broaden our outlook on life.

When something dramatically opposed to our concepts is presented for the first time, it's best not to accept or reject it at that point; unless an emergency situation demands an immediate decision of what is deemed best. Otherwise, it's sensible to set it aside briefly until our ego is at rest and we are in a more contemplative or receptive mood

Accepting anything new may mean discarding something already firmly in place and this can disrupt habitual mental and physical patterns. When this transfer is done quickly, the psychological burden may be too much for us to handle without adverse effects.

When information received is not totally perfect, we should retain what is correct and not reject the data completely. To do otherwise, would be to exhibit neurotic tendencies of illusionary perfection. The old clinker 'all or nothing at all' went out long ago with the 'Model T Ford.' As discovery of new knowledge grows, concepts must keep pace so society and science can be reasonably balanced and functional. The reliability of concepts generated by hearsay, written or oral, from past to present must be subjected to proven factors. To do less, we would be accepting or dealing with myths and illusions that imprisons the mind with a false sense of security and leaves us vulnerable to all sorts of mind manipulations. Logic takes more brainpower then that of memorization but it is the steering wheel that maneuvers us around the obstacles in life.

Until the key of relativity is used to unlock our thinking, we would be much like a dog chasing its own tail.

Embraced by logic are the three sciences of philosophy; natural, moral and metaphysical. But as with all else, the depth of logic is also limited, for it too, must compensate for evolutionary change and the continuous expanding of our consciousness.

We owe it to society that the highest degree of logic is maintained. If there is something that cannot be proven easily than steps of research should be taken before affirming it This endeavor is always worthwhile because a step toward truth is also one for enlightenment. There is more to life than following the 'flock' and watching the world go by. On the

other hand we should not be overwhelmed by words constructive and progressive for no one begins life, building skyscrapers. The words here are generally used as a projection of whatever our personal goal may be. Whenever positive action is taken, it will reward us in a reciprocating manner. It must be understood that if approached from the negative side this action will follow the same pattern that was initiated.

A mythical example of this is what happened to a small group of our humans at the dawn of civilization. A ladder fell from a cloud and a loud voice uttered these words, "This ladder has ten rungs and each one that you climb will signify a higher level of civilization. There is a problem though, one of the fellows in my workshop named, Satan, accidentally broke the bottom rung but I figured it might be a good fix it experience for you." The group assured the Voice it was no problem that they would get their heads together and draw up plans to fix the rung. So they each drew up a plan and took a vote on which one to use. "Houston" we have a small glitch here, they all voted for their own plan and there will be a further discussion on the matter. All night long and into the morning hours there was still no agreement and with egos becoming unglued, fights soon broke out. We have been killing each other ever since and the ladder still has a broken bottom rung. Ah yes, this is civilized progression.

QUESTIONING RELIGIOUS TRADITION

(It is historical proof that nearly every era produced militant Christians bent on destroying others of dissimilar views)

For ages we have struggled with the mystery of life along with a common concept of the First Cause. However, with all diverse factors surrounding it, a compatible consensus seems improbable. Most every faction professing divinely inspired truths, continue to ignore convictions of others. This generates friction and hate that eventually produces all the horrible things that we inflict on one another.

Christians like to believe they were a martyred people much longer than was the case. With the exception of a few religious leaders that the Roman Emperors considered dangerous at the time, there were only five years total, from 303-304 A.D. and 306-310 A.D. that Christians were persecuted in groups for their beliefs. From hence, however, when rulers favored Christians and they became a majority power, the situation was reversed. Then those not of Christians belief were persecuted by the thousands nearly every following era. It is folly to consider spiritual concepts as empirical and use political clout to force them on others. Yet, this action continues today as many church leaders vie for power and wealth. The Dark Ages in history and recent religious regimes in Iran and Afghanistan leaves no doubt what it does to basic freedoms.

Anything oral or written that opposes the laws of nature and science should remain in theoretical or mythical categories and must bow to the logic at hand. The discoveries made by science have given us far greater understanding of Divine purpose than the fabricated fantasies contributed by our befuddled forbearers.

Religions have resisted proven historical or scientific data and then persecuted those whose discoveries were in opposition to their primitive beliefs. Illustrious men such as Copernicus, Galileo and others were threatened, tortured or put to death unless they rescinded the proof of their profound findings.

Ironically, the Crusader armies committed robbery, rape, and murder as they pillaged countries on the way to save Palestine from the infidels.

Salem Puritans killed hundreds by burning, crushing and hanging, on mere hearsay of suspected witchcraft.

New York and Ohio Christians slew Mormons and burned down their communities for fear of losing religious and political power.

Southern Christians enslaved, killed and persecuted those of another race. Hate and bigotry of blacks was practiced throughout the South for over a hundred years after freedom for them was proclaimed.

Today's Christians adhere to civil disobedience and violence as they harass, maim or kill people while bombing clinics on the abortion issue ignoring facts that the Old Testament God, Jehovah, ordered genocide and stoning of people to death with no regard for fetuses destroyed in the process. Is not this hypocrisy on both counts? Can love and peace ever become a reality to a people who worship this God? Should we be wary of Christian militants who glorify war by singing "Onward Christian Solders," condone violence and sanction holy wars? Why, was the ethnic cleansing and genocide of Muslims by Christians in Bosnia given such little concern by Christian communities in this country? Until our President Clinton stepped in, the bigoted silence was 'deafening.' Was it because of a different religion?

In recent years, Irish Protestants and Catholics fought each other for economic advantage. Other places too such as Israel, India, Pakistan, etc. religious conflicts have become rampant. Is religion the victim of its own rhetoric and become a tool of evil? Where does our Christian love begin or is it reserved only for those of like faith?

(I John 3:15) relates that hating another falls into the same category as murder. Hate is detrimental to both mind and body. More importantly, hate is rejected by the soul and helpful communication is cut off until this poison is removed.

Hate and Divine love cannot function in unison for they are not compatible with each other. We see clergymen on TV fan hatred in the hearts of followers on religious, political and racial issues to appease their misdirected desires for power. They do it in a subtle fashion using the devil and evil as a tool or by quotes from unproven mythical sources.

Centuries ago illiterate masses depended on the educated for answers that concerned spirituality. Now the schooled majority of most countries have the capability of researching history, religions, etc., and ability to form their own opinions. Only by comparative knowledge is it possible to close in on the truth and find out why we think as we do. Until this is realized, our mental and psychic development will remain handicapped.

To counteract a threat to their status quo, fundamentalists have done their best to downplay advanced knowledge as a new age evil.

When weaknesses in archaic thought are exposed, the common defense of most zealots turns to name calling, such as atheist, infidel, heretic, etc.

Those who believe in the possibility of a Spiritual Creator of some sort but in good conscience cannot worship the Jewish god, Jehovah and also Jesus, as divine entities, are not atheists. Nor further be condemned for rejecting Biblical myth and misconceptions that others blindly accept and are afraid to challenge.

As minds mature, childhood fantasies are discarded but when a holy value is attached to them, rational reasoning takes a 'long vacation' and most of it never returns. Are we to ignore common sense and adhere to the fantasy of Eden, when there is no scientific proof that serpents were anything else but serpents from time eternity and never had voice boxes? Are we all related to Adam and Eve? The Bible refutes this when Cain took a woman from another country to be his wife. To cover this up, some say that God didn't stop creating people after Adam and Eve. If most are not related, then why should we be condemned for Adam's sin?

For an answer to that, another 'big clinker' appears, that the whole story was symbolic. Good, if that is the case, then the physical aspects of the story are lies also, including the fig leaves. So, what is the point? Are lies then being pyramided to cover other lies? Should we too, accept the credulity of other myths that deviate from natural law? In reality, are we trying to sanctify our ignorance? It makes no sense why the gift of reason is attacked in the Bible as a sin. Is this not a prime factor for our elevation over other life? As the myth unravels, the word power 'strikes a high note.' Was guilt and fear used as weapons of control for dominion over us?

Becoming heir to the original sin of Adam was a minority concept by the controversial bishop, Augustine, around the fourth century A.D. The book of (Deuteronomy 24:16) tells us that the children should not be punished or held responsible for their father's sins. This didn't seem to deter Augustine for he still promoted his theory and condemned all those born or unborn for Adams supposed sin. This inane decision did not sit well with rank and file Christians of that era. In spite of this, he gained the final support of a corrupted Emperor, who crushed all opposition to Augustine's radical views by persecution and death.

Augustine also damned Eve for Adam's dubious sin and used this guilt to lower the elevated status that women had previously enjoyed before that. During the first few centuries A.D. women were highly respected and took an active part in the leadership of religion, politics and other capacities as well. This evidently challenged the chauvinist ego of Augustine and his desire for complete religious control.

Like the murderer Paul, Augustine was responsible for hundreds being slain but also was awarded a prestigious title of Saint. Honoring such men shows lack of credibility among the clergy of that era.

Bestowing Sainthood on these men would be like awarding Adolph Hitler, the Nobel Peace Prize.

Various religious interpretations of hell and the concept of eternal damnation don't coincide with translations in earlier languages nor can they be reconciled to have the same meaning of intent as in the ancient manuscripts. Moreover, we must concede that crippling minds by fear is among the vilest of deeds.

Furthermore, the concept of hell and martyrdom of Jesus is almost an identical copy of older Egyptian and Babylonian lore. Without this theme, however, the Christian religion would have little power over their followers.

Should we study carefully the first four books of a New Testament, many places of contradiction will be found between them. This is also evident in other portions of the Bible as well. Furthermore, because of a few wise words and some beautiful illustrations, it does not represent the Bible as a whole. The Holy Bible is full of jealousy, hate, murder, rape, robbery, drunkenness, incest, torture, lies and the whole gamut of vices. Psychologically speaking, it might make more sense to give a restricted rating to the Bible and have it removed from libraries; rather than, 'Harry Potter' or 'Lords of the Ring' books that some avid religious factions are still trying to ban? This again exemplifies the closed minds where the kid next door is considered a devil and my 'Johnny' an angel. If our brains hadn't been pickled and jarred into believing the Bible was holy, how many would now believe in the hyperbole of Biblical myths? These are good illustrations of why church and state should be separated.

Theologians constantly ignore the truths of science, historical data in other books, letters and biographies. When dealing with antiquity, rarely is the 'picture' complete and like a jig saw puzzle, bits and pieces of data are important in filling the gaps and giving us more logical answers. However, the more that is conveyed makes one believe that the stories behind the stories are the fictitious imagination of writers. Every setting must have names and places, but has no bearing on the truth of a story.

For lack of living witnesses this too is presumptuous but some factors logically outweigh others and are more probable and closer to reality. Clues from other sections of scripture relating to that era make it appear that Paul (Saul) started most of the false concepts about Jesus and was reprimanded for it by Jesus' brother, James, who was then the leader of Jesus' followers. It's obvious to those aware of the principles of cause and effect that many times the Bible confirms that Jesus and his disciples believed in reincarnation. This then would nullify Paul's fantasy of the Master's purpose here on earth. When James had Peter check on Paul, he took an immediate dislike to Peter. This was intimated with Paul's own words in one of the books attributed to him. Later, in a letter that was ascribed to Peter, he suggested to James that something should be done about the evil in their midst. With a man of Paul's temperament and conviction, it is feasible that he continued aborting the truth about Jesus, which then forced James to call a final meeting between the two. It can logically be assumed from what happened, that James relieved Paul of his missionary assignment. With Paul's huge ego and violent temper, it appeared that he reverted to his murderous ways and had his henchmen kill Jesus' brother. It's still a mystery to Biblical scholars why the Romans saved Paul from retaliation from James followers and how well he was treated as a prisoner for a short time after. The whole truth of this episode may never be known. We must face the fact that the Bible is a hodgepodge of works by scores of writers; most of it with no proven claim of authorship other then than that of hearsay. It is totally unreal to believe that all of these writers were divinely inspired on mere human hearsay of others. The entire idea of Divine inspiration becomes a paradox, for to prove it as true, only the Divine can logically make that judgment and there is no proof that God ever said a word. Concepts of a Biblical nature then, seem founded on words of illusionary 'smoke.'

By adhering strictly to what was taught, the memorizing portion of the brain becomes active and psychic help from the right hemisphere is mostly ignored. When our total reasoning abilities of one brain side is not used, it becomes weak and dysfunctional.

When accounting to balance the bottom line, inconsistencies must be challenged and by relative deductions more logical perceptions of the truth can become quite clear. A good question clarifier is 'whose axe they trying to grind'? When answers are not compatible with other data, it's ridiculous to assume their legitimacy. (For example)

Does the Son of God run amok in a temple threatening people with whips? Wouldn't this be out of character and oppose Jesus' teachings of love and forgiveness? There is a big contradiction here and an important question remains. Who injected this episode into the Bible and why?

If 'Jesus' described his Father in heaven as ever loving; was the hateful God in the Old Testament then an imposter, too?

If Jehovah gave the Biblical Ten Commandments to Moses then why would he later go against his written word, 'Love thy neighbor as thyself:' then give a genocide order for the Israelites to kill every man, woman and child with the exception of virgins when they moved in to capture a land that for centuries was inhabited by others? Also the commandment, 'Thou shall not kill' then to promote stoning family members to death for disobedience to their parents. Were we duped into worshipping a false war god?

We must realize that many years ago the only known light at night would be that of the moon or a fire. Could the episode of the burning bush that was not consumed, have been that of an artificial light emitted by an alien craft? In many years past, there have been legends of these ships, pictures of them cut in stone, references of them in East Indian sacred books and even remains of what appear to be landings sites in S. America.

Could the Greek myths have been actual sightings of these craft on Mount Olympus and its occupants also deemed to be gods?

Interesting is it not, that these vehicles followed the exodus of the Israelites from Egypt and appeared as smoke or vapor trails during the day and fire or light by night? Is it possible that Yahweh was an alien also, and had the expertise to part the waters for the Israelites to escape?

There are at least three possible variations of the exodus story to explore and many points appear more valid than others. It all makes the story more interesting to talk about for many incidents in the exodus story appear exaggerated or downright fiction. When Moses gave the signal with his staff that all had crossed the sea safely, did the aliens then let the waters reunite? Not that it really happened in this way but the references made of these craft in historical books other than the Bible, makes some things seem more probable. Producing more than one explanation will drive perfectionists 'bananas' for to them there can only be one answer.

The pact Jehovah made with the Israelites and how an ark of the covenant was constructed for voice communication with Him is very significant. If the Hebrew god were also considered Creator of the universe, would it be sane to believe that an ultimate Divine Being needed a mechanical contraption to communicate? Are we being used for someone else's glorification? A Creator God needs no glorification nor has to prove Self to anyone for the Divine would be glory absolute. Is it merely the vanity of man's ego that surmises us to be made in God's image? If the Creator of all things including the many universes were to walk the earth, would not the power of His radiance be more than a thousand suns and far too brilliant for human eyes to behold?

If longevity of some concept is considered proof of credibility, must we pay homage to ignorance because it has been around much longer than all else? Has our civilization regressed to the point that we would rather continue to kill one another then try to think?

Change can be devastating to some because of losing illusionary security to which our minds have become adapted. But what may be even more disastrous is the act of ignoring basic truths and having never realized the joy of being able to share a cup of 'spiritual tea' with our true self. Before we begin meditating to find our true selves, a 'window' in our mind must be opened to allow rhetoric and hearsay a chance to escape and evaporate into the nothingness from whence it came. We can then acknowledge a 'knock at the door' and accept the invitation to an esoteric meeting, uninterrupted by the rabble of traditional ghosts.

THE RELIGIOUS PARADOX

(In the early days of religion, anathemas or so called curses were dished out as regular as a bowl of soup)

The intention of this chapter is not to convey religion in an entirely negative light, but to portray both sides of the spectrum as truthful as possible. Judgment of its value is left to the conscience level of each individual. Its purpose is to reflect on the lack of relativity in human perception of certain accepted concepts.

Though great strides have been achieved in many modern agendas, we have ignored the application of historical and scientific data to update traditional beliefs. To reverse this trend it is important to recognize our need of equalizing esoteric beliefs with that of known factors. We are now an educated people and must rationalize ancient superstitions and myths that served as a security blanket for naïve ancestors. The growing gap between fantasy and reality is getting wider with every new era and this can only promote hatred and escalate more wars.

The indulged notion of us having reached a level of intelligence far above past civilizations has little credence when we still cling to old age beliefs that have no proof or scientific logic. The danger of separating ourselves into groups of like thought from the rest of society can only breed suspicion and contempt toward others. Biased conformity stirs up prejudice and resentment of other views. As this bigotry deepens, the friction and hate it creates will eventually erupt into all sorts of violent confrontations.

Ironically, fact and logic that could improve these weaknesses are pushed aside. Much of this stems from political apathy to deal with fact and truth in many areas for fear of emotional feedback that might puts dents in the prevailing power structure. If facts in new discoveries are not fully acted upon at primary levels we are apt to drift back to relying on the status quo.

From then on our society may continue to pass outmoded data to future generations and to some extent the dark ages remain again for some time to come. These form traditional thoughts and customs that can become roadblocks to the necessary progress for our social needs.

Though rigidly denied by the orthodox establishment, their concepts remain firmly rooted to superstitions of our pagan ancestors. Proof of this may be found in countless sources of historical data. Even a high school student would have little difficulty in researching and affirming this fact. To maintain control, many religions dote on the ignorance and insecurity of people by projecting a fictional guilt and an illusionary fix to a solution for redemption. This type of religious mind control creeps into public government as well, whereby laws and mores of a general nature are created to coincide with concepts of various religious beliefs.

Other than natural law, truth in our dimension is not an actuality but a growing element of consciousness. Most religions assume theirs to be pristine and the only accurate one. Some take their scriptures literally, while others combine allegorical interpretations with their reasoning. This gives us a myriad of different views and as many sects of opposing opinions. It could be said that religion is a political arm of spirituality, where an attempt is made to consolidate thought into a biased common denominator. This then gives religious leaders greater control and an umbrella of power in which to operate.

Ideas and views of a few are formulated into rigid creeds and tenets that members are avowed to live by. Those who question or stray from the invented precepts are then often chastised and/or ostracized for their freedom of thought.

For one reason or another, religion fills a psychological need for many of us that seek a sense of spirituality and the feel of security that flocking engenders.

This shouldn't be denied those who wish to reinforce their comfort zones in this manner. However, when religions convey perfection of so called 'holy books' friction is bound to surface with others who may also deem their books in like esteem. The opposing egos will eventually clash for they can't all be right. Unless, there is a desire to be a martyr, it's best to flee from the grip of spiritual leaders that use the evil tools of guilt and fear to control us.

There is no sane reason for anyone to worship a Hebrew god called Yahweh or Jehovah. Dropping sacrosanct fantasy surrounding the story of creation, the best to be assumed, is that Yahweh created the Jewish race from his own genetics that reflected an image likeness and give the impression of being one of a chosen race. Now, if Yahweh is the only one and true God according to the Old Testament, then we are saying that the Master of the Universe has all the negative weaknesses of the humans, such as prejudice, discrimination, envy, hate, revenge, etc. Wouldn't disrespect of this nature be utter blasphemy?

A great error in the Jews primitive thinking was the misconception that Jehovah was Elohim, creator of heaven and earth. The jealousy, anger, hate and murder in Yahweh' heart was ghastly. Jews feared him because his violent rage and revenge for disobedience was awesome and sadistic at times. This madness extended to his unholy order of genocide for another people, whom he also presumably created. It is ironic that this God did not honor his own commandments and even promoted the stoning of relatives to death for acts of disobedience. Then there were the curses so debase in temperament and revenge that they went beyond individual punishment to include relatives and heirs for generations to come. This impostor posing as the Creator God was an obvious fraud; yet the Christian church later coerced members into accepting this very negative being as Creator of the universe. How totally 'uncool.'

Nowhere, do the actions of Yahweh coincide with Jesus' portrayal of the Heavenly Father, in a parable of the prodigal son or the teaching of Jesus to forgive seventy times seven. There is no logical reasoning to justify accepting our Creator and this Yahweh as the same entity. If the Christians believe Jesus to be the Son of God, how can any lesser being that contradicts His theme of Divine love ever be considered? Wouldn't this be sheer hypocrisy? Why, in spite of the holocaust's horrible results, do Jews remain loyal to a genocide god? Is it fear and their bigotry that are working together here? Could the holocaust be some sort of racial karma the Jews had to endure because of their allegiance to Yahweh? It should be realized that the universal law of cause and effect (what we sow, shall we reap) applies to the creative forces of thought as well as those of action.

There is no wrong in professing one's faith in a humble manner, for the purity of intent outweighs many factors. But, if our attitudes bear the signs of aloofness and self-righteousness, then we are like the Biblical Pharisees; who paraded their virtues in public, were critical of others and separated themselves from supposed inferiors.

Some religious philosophies are postured like instant food and drink and by merely uttering a few words, it qualifies us for a 'free piggyback' ride to the 'rosy hereafter' as it were.

When we succumb to a concept, it becomes an ego battlefield and any proof contrary to the ideal will rarely change our mind. Admitting to shortcomings in our beliefs shouldn't lessen self-esteem for error is the necessary ingredient for personal growth. Truth in knowledge is always ongoing and should be a satisfying experience and can remain so the rest of our lives if approached with the right attitude.

Thankfully, the art of living isn't 'cut in stone' for it would be really boring if it were so.

Emotional ignorance should never dominate logic that stimulates a positive attitude of mind and the growth of character. A relative factor retarding this growth, in many cases, has been repressive actions of rigid theologies to orientate young minds away from the freedom of thought. They wind up parroting religious rhetoric while specifics of fact finding are ignored. All too often, when the door to knowledge is open to free the captive mind, it refuses to leave an illusionary security of our mental prison. This action is not to be chastised or pitied for we are responsible for choices made which guide our destinies.

Though we may not be aware of cosmic consciousness at a certain point in life, it's still within, waiting for recognition. Biblical reference of 'lost soul' is taken out of context and given an erroneous meaning. If our soul is of a divine essence then logically it must also be eternal. It is possible to lose contact with our soul for a time but the real us is never lost and eventually must return to its original source where future plans for further development may be in store for us. Taken out of context is the fabrication of hell and the messianic martyrdom; all are duplications of past events in historical lore of other countries, long before the New Testament was written. Check out Egyptian and Babylonian history and lore, for instance, before we become entrenched with adamant views.

If fear or apathy deters us from searching for factual answers, the truth that we are capable of knowing, will escape us and we will keep tripping over our man made righteousness. Very few study the origin of their religions or the concepts of other faiths. The information received is most often gleaned from biased opinions or prejudiced hearsay. More time is usually spent on specifics of buying a car or choosing a wardrobe than on the esoteric values that are supposed to determine the quality of our eternal life. Many are taught to rely on decisions of others where matters of spiritual importance are concerned. Usually, those giving advice adhere to questionable old concepts that were seldom challenged.

One of the most inane actions of religions is sending missionaries to preach their refined guesswork to gullible people who are less educated. For the most part, those chosen to be missionaries are naïve but good people when it comes to zealous dedication and unselfish sacrifice.

Many take with them important skills that can benefit those they are about to serve. The negative part of their act comes about when attempts are made to supplant the spirituality of others with that of their own.

As an example, it may begin something like this. We have a young man that was brought up in a Christian neighbor hood and attended the Christian schools. It was natural to absorb the same spiritual views of his parents that had been passed down for generations. Then too, in the parochial schools he attended, necessary literature of scientific value was often ignored if it didn't conform to mythical beliefs. Through formative years, it was impressed upon him that literature and thought that opposed his faith was false and the tainted work of Satan. This tactic was another means to control minds so a biased faith would not be questioned and its authority could remain intact. Though it sounds ridiculous, this practice, none-the-less, is still a survival technique of many religions today.

Before becoming a missionary, however, the young man would have to attend a seminary for more 'brain washing' where the spirituality was based primarily on creeds of his religion or denomination. Any data that opposed those views were suppressed or omitted without valid research or honest clarification. But, at that point, it really didn't matter, because his mindset was already firmly established. After graduation he was now prepared to spread the word of man, falsely classified as God's, word to those backward people who had not yet been exposed to their religion's doctrine. The object was to convert people to his holy brand of religious hearsay, unchanged for centuries as an assumed truth. And to give it more clout, Biblical writers would infer that God said this or that, all of which was an unproven myth and fantasy of pagan minds.

When this was questioned by more learned people, religionists went out on a limb to say that they were inspired by the Holy Spirit to relay this or that message. And this worked out quite well for a time because nobody got close enough to the Holy Spirit to ask him if that was so. The fact is that the Biblical words were either spoken or written by man and there is no proof that a Creator ever gave anyone the authority to represent his mind. There is no proof that God ever spoke a word and He still is silent on that subject or any other for that matter.

In the next few pages a scenario will be enacted to demonstrate the irrational thought and behavior in past religious practices. Among other things it brings to light an orthodox disrespect for the spiritual heritage of others. Before the arrival of foreigners the natives were perfectly happy worshipping the sun, a symbol of their deity. Upon his arrival, however, the new missionary deemed all this sun worship as sinful. Inhabitants were told that the real symbol of God now rested on a paper book with words written by people none of the islanders knew or the missionary either, for the matter. This radical idea was deemed superior to God's beautiful handiwork, so they were told to forget the sun.

This Bible as it was called, was the greatest because it was written by lots of authors inspired by a Holy Spirit. Holy didn't make much of an impression on the natives but when the word Spirit hit their ears, fear shone in their eyes and they started paying attention because they had a superstition that there were a lot of spirits roaming the hills in their area. It was stressed that if they refused to believe all that was spoken by this man of the cloth, a curse would befall them. Religious authors of early times dished out anathemas (curses) as regular as a 'bowl of soup,' on those who didn't believe what they said.

Now, if there happened to be a neighboring missionary competing for lost souls, the natives were told to believe only the true messenger of God, now speaking before them.

The screwed up fellow of another faith should be ignored for the poor man was obviously under the influence of Satan.

Oh yes, Satan, the big daddy evil spirit had to be introduced to the native mind as quickly as possible. You couldn't hide from him either, for he had eyes in the back of his head and always knew where you were. To make matters worse this creature was invisible to boot. And it didn't stop here because this guy was not like the regular evil spirits who paid the natives a once in lifetime visit when the volcano blew its top. No sir, this joker hung around every day of the year. And, he wasn't about to be outdone by nagging little demons that showed up occasionally during the night either, for this sucker never slept. If he didn't zap you during the night, you had to worry about him looking over your shoulder all day long, to 'boot.'

The big clincher came when they were told about the big volcano up in the sky that's called hell! Now, if they didn't repent and do as told by the missionary, this inferno awaits them after death and they would then be burned in hell. And just so sinners wouldn't forget what they were there for, 'forever' was added to the threat. When one native asked, if you were caught in a fire on earth and were burned to death; how could you be burned to death the second time in hell? It was explained to the doubting 'Thomas' that you cannot burn a soul and this proxy, as it were, is what must take all this suffering in hell.

This raised an eyebrow by a youngster in the crowd and he quipped, "Now if the soul can't be burned on earth, then why in hell do they try to do the same thing? This small heretic was put on an isolated island three days without food or water for swearing and had to stay there until he repented or got his head on straight, which ever came first, of course. The natives too, were constantly reminded how fortunate it was that explorers had discovered them or they all would have been doomed to this horrible hell.

Further more, this put the natives forever in debt to the missionaries for saving their rotten, worthless souls from eternal damnation. Then in conclusion, after all this fear had been properly instilled into the minds of the trembling inhabitants, they were told to go home, be happy and have a good day.

Expressing things candidly is often necessary to clearly expose the absurd weaknesses in religious attitudes. Though some portrayals may not have been the norm or various details exaggerated a bit; it strays not far from practices of today's religions. The sad part is that this same arrogance still remains a common denominator of many religious sects. As in previous eras, insolence shown toward those of differing views, are still big contributors to social miseries and past or present wars.

In retrospect, if we were a poor people and some wealthier nation tried to win our children over to their religious belief with bribes of gifts, candy and favors, would our reactions be any different than those taken against us? Sanctimonious leaders prefer the word 'converting' instead of 'interfering' when referring to their specific missions. They also want our government to protect them from any animosity against them for the agitation they have created.

Anyone endeavoring communication with others need much more knowledge than most 'one track' minds have to offer. How can anyone with a 'hat on backwards' be diversified when they spend half their time hiding under a table from Satan and the other half praying to an Old Testament genocide God. Can those living in fear think freely and act responsibly? The best way clergy can help society is by first cleaning out their religious 'closets.' This would entail facing reality, quit taking things out of context and conducting 'open end' discussions concerning spirituality. The world is becoming more knowledgeable and you cannot cover up the truth much longer. If you don't do it now, you will lose it all and be eternally condemned as liars. Another good method would be to stand on your wobbly legs and sanction peace over war.

As with all else, when power and wealth become a motivating force in religion, the corruption trail will follow. Religions then come under the sway of the very forces it touts as its enemy. True spirituality cannot be found in a book, adopted from the tongue of another nor secured in a place of worship. Spirituality begins within our inner temple where the presence of cosmic love abides in every soul. Literally, we must let no one lead us from a 'personal contact' with the 'First Cause' and restrict us from entering the universal temple of knowledge and love..

Many believe prayer is like meditation but this cannot be for the ego is always present to some extent as prayer is a personal plea. Prayer can have a temporary comforting effect for it is usually tied to our concepts. Meditation, however, is the key for receiving impressions and answers from the inner self that will help give our lives more meaning. From this perspective it is strange at first to those who rely heavily on the memory guidance system of past programming by others. In meditation at first our interpretations will not be errorless per se; but there will come a time as the psychic develops, so too will our accuracy for it is a prime mover of our real eternal self. Doing our 'homework' as best we can is an only cosmic requirement for an enlightened journey.

The religion we were taught to believe as perfect in formative years may have provided a catalyst against other misplaced fears. However, as adults, we must eventually come to grips with a revelation that the main source of creation is love and our 'pipe line' to this source originates in the soul. Should any curse or veiled threat appear in the scriptures of our present belief, be aware of two things. That it was a fabrication by some past writer or conveyed by a false prophet with an ulterior motive. As discussed in previous chapters there may be errors in interpretations, poor adaptations, translations, editing, printing etc. of our most cherished and respected literature. We must push aside the negatively erected ego barriers and learn to accept what shows to be predominantly logical fact.

Do not be surprised when this changes from time to time as our wisdom grows and this is as it should be.

Regardless of the many imperfections that are encountered in our literature, there is usually something positive that can be gleaned from it. Though taught to strive for perfection and admire what it's imagined to be, it only extends to limits of our perception and remains an illusionary goal. Without imperfection and error there could never be our learning experiences on earth and this would logically nullify the purpose of our existence. Projection of evil is also necessary as a comparative tool to determine the quality of what is good. That is not to mean we should actively become part of the negative, unless of course, a lesson to be learned has a temporary value. Therein lies the difficulty to entertain an accurate judgment on the action of others. Although not obvious to us at times, there may be many progressive factors involved.

As evidenced by actions of nature and confirmed through scientific study, we can logically conclude its laws to be evolutionary and stable. Contrary to popular superstitions, God or the cosmic will not intercede in breaking the natural laws. Volcanoes will continue to erupt, earthquakes move and seas flood according to cosmic plan. What personal suffering that is experienced may be contingent on past or present involvement with the universal law of cause and effect. We suffer this effect when we break some natural law and it has nothing to do with holy revenge or the decided involvement of a supernatural being. This would revert back to archaic superstitions of pagan ancestors. If God is creative and all knowing, then anger and vengeance could not be a part of his character. In our ignorance we try to perceive ourselves as made in God's image. This is the result of an inflated ego trying to sanctify our weaknesses and negative attributes. In the first place, why would a divine unlimited spirit limit his being to an earthly human body with all kinds of limitations?

Think about it for a minute, an eagle can see better then us, a dog can smell better, a deer can hear better, fish can swim better, birds can fly better and at times we stink. Just one phrase, says it all; 'what fools we mortals be!'

Miracles too are not supernatural interventions but the effects of natural law that have yet to be understood. Jesus suggested this in the Bible when questioned about miracles and said 'that this you can do also and more' but Christians seem reluctant to drop pagan beliefs and accept this fact. We humans seem content with implanted fears and mythical superstitions than to practice relative thinking and logical reasoning.

If for security reasons, religion is important in helping us maintain a spiritual equilibrium of some sort, then by all means let it become part of our comfort zone. However, allowing our spiritual awareness to progress to a higher level of consciousness would be much more gratifying, for this engenders a greater respect and closer union with cosmic sources.

- An eminent philosopher once stated that -

TO THE SOULS THAT FEED ON THE BREAD OF LIFE, OUTWARD CONVENTIONS OF RELIGION ARE NO LONGER NEEDFUL.

HID WITH THE CHRIST (CONSCIOUSNESS) IN GOD, THERE IS FOR THEM, SMALL PLACE FOR OUTWARD RITES,

FOR ALL EXPERIENCE IS A HOLY BAPTISM,

A PERPETUAL SUPPER WITH THE LORD

AND ALL LIFE IS SACRIFICE, HOLY AND ACCEPTABLE TO GOD.

_____?_____ Roundtree

LOGIC AND SCIENCE

(Noah and the Ark is one of the biggest Biblical farces and is also substantiated by science and common sense)

The sanest reason we exist in our dimension is for the opportunities to learn, otherwise, the value of our purpose on earth would appear to be 'faceless.' How we adapt to situations using available knowledge reflects upon intellectual progress. Value in wisdom relies on the depth of our awareness to an actuality of truth; for the absolute state of truth is not yet unattainable by the human mind. However, a positive feature to this, are the many facets to explore while searching for answers that will continue to open more doors to a greater reality. Knowledge is temporal and is relative to our expanding consciousness and they must evolve together.

The downside to human progress is the implementation of illusionary fears that acts like a virus to the mind. This keeps us from thinking in a rational and healthy manner. Fear and hate feed off one another and an animal is more likely to attack when either of these signals is present. In other words, illusionary fears have created sick minds that are unable to function within their capabilities. Fear for control purposes is the most hideous of crimes and the practice of such should be a forbidden issue with any sane and civilized society. In this respect it is evident that our societies have a long way to go.

Vanity of status and assets are negative delusions and when they hit the fan of reality they are blown away like dust. Adhering to concepts of others based on mere hearsay stifles the impetus to question, search and analyze from relative viewpoints. Fear of the unknown and clinging to imaginary security, we are reluctant to change our views even when advanced knowledge is presented.

The greatest stumbling blocks of human progress must eventually point to traditional and orthodox thought. The logic thereof is based on assumed truths and hearsay of ancient writers whose 'attics' were loaded with 'cobwebs of superstition' that was inherited from pagan ancestors.

With the advances of science many religious concepts are exposed as nothing more than superstitions and myths that should have died in the era of their origin. Science then becomes an enemy to religion because it challenges the security of programmed minds that believe in something literal as the word of God. Man wrote every word of the Bible with no evidence of our Creator's permission to represent the Divine Mind. Any opposition to invented myths are then erroneously regarded as an attack on the Divine and deemed blasphemous. The gravest error is not what we wish to believe which is everyone's right, but the subtle means of fear which is used to cripple minds and discourage freedom of thought. Evil perpetrators have always used fear to control others and this method is still prevalent in religions today.

As the gap between religion and science keeps widening, orthodox factions are now making a last ditch stand from falling apart. They're desperately trying to incorporate religion into government affairs and public institutions of learning. Logic backed by known factors has little impact on their traditional beliefs.

Take for example, the tale of Noah and the Ark. On a recent TV show religious zealots were all agog over a discovery of something on Mount Ararat that may have been Noah's ark. This to them would then substantiate the complete story of the ark as true. Even though there may have been an ark and a flood of some kind, circumstances surrounding the episode cannot be justified by historical and scientific data.

When the ark story originated, it's apparent that people of the area had no awareness of the continents or how vast the earth actually was. Their world concepts centered on territory bordering the Mediterranean Sea and a few countries beyond. The flood was said to cover the entire earth and from Biblical genealogy charts it must have taken place within the last five thousand years. Over the ages, the world had many floods, proven by the clay varves that were formed after each flood receded.

There is no scientific evidence, however, confirming that a flood of universal proportions ever took place during this period in time. A flood of such magnitude would not only affect the status and composition of clay varves the world over but of many other things relative to various environment conditions as well. Then too, archaeological and geological studies have shown that since the continent of Atlantis submerged, an estimated 11,000 years ago, the position of the others have seen little major change.

The most recent discoveries place the Egyptian civilization within a few thousand years after the Atlantis disaster. Since that time, Egyptians and their culture remained intact; proof thereof indelibly cut in stone on temple walls, pillars, tombs, etc. With help of the Rosetta stone more recent discoveries keep pushing the Egyptian civilization back further into antiquity than was generally anticipated.

To surmise that everyone on earth is now all related to Noah's family is absurd. A leopard does not change its spots overnight nor would people change into diverse races in five thousand years. The Egyptians have been the same race for over 10,000 years and this can logically be concluded for other races as well.

The Biblical story stated that this huge flood covered the whole earth and necessitated that all living creatures in pairs to be saved and put on the ark. God's instructions to Noah also included taking aboard the necessary food to feed all these creatures for a year. Let reason and known factors take over and analyze the consequences of the directions. This would include indigenous creatures from every part of the world and many territories had not even been discovered yet. They would have had to be trapped or captured and then transported by ships and countless caravans to reach the ark's location. Common sense tells us that many creatures were not adapted to water, to climb over mountains, traverse deserts or overcome conditions that were foreign to their habitat.

Transportation efforts back then would be an impossible task as the sailing ships were incredibly small and slow at that time and caravans had to maintain a speed of foot travel. Animals and men had to be fed along the way and this would present additional problems. Ships and caravans would number into the hundreds plus thousands of men to handle the arduous task of loading and unloading during various journey transfers. Not only would it have involved a national effort but world support as well. How could this be achieved when during construction of the ark, there was very little support even from Noah's own people?

We must now visualize kangaroos, koalas, ostriches, wild dogs, etc. from Australia: bison, elk, moose, deer, mountain sheep, grizzlies, polar bears, wolves, pumas etc. from N. America: Llamas, monkeys, jaguars, peccaries, constrictors etc. from S. America: Yaks, horses, elephants, Brahman cattle, tigers, monkeys, etc. from Asia: Lions, leopards, water buffalo, hyenas, giraffes, rhinos, gazelles, etc. from Africa. After the flood most animals would have to be transported back to their original habitats. We couldn't expect a kangaroo to hop across two continents and swim the Pacific back to Australia.

Holding pens and cages would have had to be built to separate the species, not only in route to the ark, but also once aboard; otherwise, many in the natural food chain would be missing the next day. These lost inventories might have to be replaced from half way around the world. In that case, the guy standing gang plank watch may have a hard time staying awake until replacements came aboard.

According to the story, it was over a year before God gave Noah permission to release all land creatures from the ark. Now, to feed all these animals their natural diets for over a year while on the ark was not possible. For instance, it would entail adequate supplies of fresh bamboo shoots for the pandas, eucalyptus for the koalas and likewise for various diets of other creatures aboard.

There would have to be more than pairs of the smaller animals for the diets of the larger carnivores consisted of flesh from the weaker ones.

The diets of smaller animal would require an even much greater variety.

Now an elephant alone consumes about 375 lbs of vegetation a day and a pair would need 750 lbs. Multiply this for a year aboard the ark and Noah would have had to load aboard 190 tons of hay or grass for just this one pair of animals. A conservative estimate of food for the other vegetarians aboard would put it upward of 3000 tons. Balers had not yet been invented so all the fodder would have to be cut, loaded on wagons and then stacked aboard the ark; all of this done by hand. Now, ask any farmer how many football fields it would take to free stack 3000 tons of hay. It would be suffice to say that such a volume would be enough to bury a dozen arks or more regardless of their height.

Then, of course, we must not forget that carnivorous animals were also to be fed. With no refrigeration, thousands of sheep or animals for meat on the hoof must be kept on board to provide this necessity. This livestock would require countless more tons of feed while alive.

This is just the tip of the iceberg; for besides feeding tons of food to the animals every day, tons of manure must be removed. It is doubtful there were enough people in Noah's family to handle all these chores, even working 24 hr. days. If the Bible is labeled the word of God, who is lying; God or some inspired writers? Most Christians believe the story literally while some put an allegorical tag on it and both fall flat. All of the alibis and arguments supporting this fictional story have been more ridiculous than the tale itself. Rationale that exposes the false conclusions of the ark myth can aptly apply to other Biblical myths as well. This would include the Garden of Eden, Jonah and the whale, along with other mentioned miracles. There are also a myriad of misconceptions and errors in the bible that most of us ignore for fear of challenging something in a book that is deemed as holy.

To cover up the most exaggerated tales of the Bible and deter being questioned by sensible people, these stories were classified as miracles. This eliminated further discussion, for anyone to question a supernatural act, would be declared sacrilegious. When belief in something as holy, the mind goes on a vacation and seems to get lost on the way back.

Many psychologists have concluded that regardless of the education, most of us rarely think for ourselves. We have become dependent on the memorizing portion of the brain and become pedant on the information stored there. A good memory is important but only 'half the loaf' as it were. If memory portions of data are in error, results will reflect the same. The psychic half produces an overall picture to help the analyzing half of the brain with comparisons. Without correlation of two halves we are apt to considered halfwits by intelligent observers.

An academic weakness has been that of teaching what to think with little emphasis on the importance of how to think. Because of this, many of us shy from critical thinking and we are apprehensive to approach the cutting edge of our thinking abilities. Most of us

function primarily from past memories, cling to traditional rhetoric and mimic the thought and action of others for the flocking security we feel in numbers. The only way out of this self imposed, 'squirrel cage' is become better acquainted with our inner self, for therein lie the clues to why we think as we do. Otherwise, the cataract of ignorance will continue to blur our vision to the world of reality when faced with the necessity of compensating or changing our views. Reversing the significance we once placed on past values may seemingly give our life a worthless meaning. This too is merely an illusion, for we have learned and accomplished many positive things in life, even while toting unnecessary burdens around with us much of the time. Rigid conventions, established in our minds, have a tendency to keep pushing logic aside.

Even if a truth did not manifest itself until our last day on earth, it would still make our journey worthwhile.

Varied attitudes are best viewed with patience, just as the cosmic is with us; for every soul has a blueprint to work out and no other mortal has access to another's timetable. Until we rationalize superstitions or myth for what they are, hope for an enlightened civilization will also remain a myth.

Trying to replace science with superstition and fantasy is regressive and non-productive. Although our human conceptions are not perfect, science still produces most logical answers based on analytical research and fact finding at their point in time. Another plus is sciences' ability to update its original concepts when a newer discovery proves to be more accurate. Flexibility is necessary in the process of refining knowledge but this fact usually takes a 'back seat' to the egos steeped in orthodox traditions.

We continually delude ourselves into thinking that there are quick answers to most things and an attainment to some sort of perfection here on earth. Yet, it's quite obvious that this world was not designed as a heaven or it would be one. It's natural to be uncomfortable not

knowing answers to questions we deem important but if we are not consciously prepared for them, the side effects could be more painful. An element of wonder will keep our minds active and pointed in a positive direction. By raising our awareness to a higher level of consciousness we must be able to think relatively and this cannot hurt us. The only pain we are apt to suffer is from a bruised ego.

The Book of Errors

(The exodus of the Israelites from the land of Egypt is a close second to the fabrication of Noah and the ark.)

We all are imperfect humans whose opinions may be in error and reflect the quality from which our knowledge was obtained. All that was written or conveyed is from human creations and abstract illusions. Yet, when a book is deemed 'holy' (a human qualification based on fantasy) reasoning or logic based on the contents are seldom questioned because of ignorance and fear. Difference to any portion would then be deemed blasphemy and subject to an erroneous act of Divine retribution. To begin, many errors can be found in the first Biblical books, for Old Testament writers seemed adept at story telling and their imaginations went wild in distorting the specifics of non-witnessed events. It was a common practice among opposing factions then to prove their invented God was mightier than all others.

Following Jacob and his family into Egypt and what occurred in the next five hundred years is enough not only to question the story's validity but many of the other Biblical incidents as well. What is related in some of the following paragraphs and other places in this chapter were gleaned from a very reputable modern source by Bruce Feiler, the author of a book entitled "Walking the Bible" and is most revealing of errors in the Old Testament. His book is a must in reading for any serious biblical scholar. What gives the book classic proportion was additional expertise and knowledge furnished by a famed archeologist of the Middle East who accompanied the author virtually every step of the way on his journey through 'Holy Land' territory.

During a famine, Jacob's family, numbering seventy people, went to Egypt and were allowed to live in the land of Goshen. They were not considered slaves until much later when under a different Pharaoh they were forced to give up a certain percentage of what they produced and also refused exit from the country.

After 430 years in Egypt, the Biblical estimate of the adult Israelite male population was over six hundred thousand. Now there must have been an equal number or more of women and after counting the children it would bring the figure to well over two million Israelites. There are some who have calculated that this many people would have constituted a good proportion of the lower Nile's population and a force not to be ignored. Though figures are moot and may vary with different sources the scope appears to be significant. With the migration of such a large number of people, one might reason that this vacancy would have been noticed and recorded in the history of trading countries but no such proof of this can be found.

As mentioned in Feiler's book, the Israelites were supposed to have crossed the Red Sea but according to the Hebrew language they crossed the yam suf, yam meaning sea and suf signifying reed. Suf, could also be a derivative from the Egyptian word swf that means papyrus. In this case, papyrus cannot grow in salt water, which the Red Sea is comprised of. This being true, then most likely one of the bitter lakes was crossed and Lake Timsah, could have been the most logical one, for it was shallow and certain areas could be waded through but any horse and chariot would surely get bogged down. The Israelites wouldn't take the

northern route for it was fortified against invaders and might also present an obstacle to their exit. So presumably, they crossed the water further south into the Sinai desert and spent the next forty years there before moving into the land of Canaan. A number of speculations and many questions remain unanswered about the Israelite exodus from Egypt and we may never for sure the true story in every detail. However, the book of Jasher appears to be much more authentic than other versions for it was written by the author who was also an eye witness to all of the main events that took place, even during the capture of Canaan. Jasher was the fourth Israel leader in line from Moses, Joshua, Caleb, then himself.

Events were recorded just as they were observed with no personal opinions Jasher might have concerning them. As a ruler, he was loved and known by his people as an upright and truthful person. His book was mentioned in two places in the Holy Bible; Joshua 10:13 and 2nd Samuel 1:18. It was considered lost, however, during a Babylonian invasion. A wealthy Englishman, Alcuin, was interested in the Mid-east Holy Land and set out with two Hebrew translators on a journey there in the late eight century A.D. After about three years of visiting dozens of cities and places along the way, including Palestine, he stumbled upon information that a scroll existed in the small town of Gazna, in northern Persia, that could possibly be the lost book of Jasher, that was referred to in the Bible. After bribing several officials with wedges of gold, he was then allowed to examine and copy an exceptionally preserved papyrus manuscript with a white flexible backing about a quarter of an inch thick.

Alcuin and his translators took up residence there until the chore was finished which took about eight years. They stopped in Rome on the way back to England to show the Pope and he applauded it as a great find. The Pope was in his eighties and had a failing memory so he was told them to take it back to England and show it to trusted authorities there until such time that it can be recopied and revealed to the public. . Alcuin eventually gave the book to a friend for safekeeping and nothing more was heard about it until centuries later when discovered again in northern England around 1750. This is very significant for it was after the printing press was invented If not for this, the material may have been hand copied many times and changed to suit or conform to the rigid and already established theologies of the day, thus losing its authenticity. but because of time factors and writer's I.D. we must recognize this book as the earliest, and most valued book of the Bible. Being written by the fourth ruler of Israel who witnessed what happened every step of the way makes Jasher's book an incomparable classic of authority.

After the original book was lost, later writers attempted to fill the historical gap with their invented versions of what happened at that time. Though the book of Jasher was highly approved by religious authorities in England, they were reluctant to make it a permanent part of the Canon scripture. The book was put in and taken out of the Bible several times before the church hierarchy deemed that its contents too controversial. It would embarrass the status quo to change anything that happened in the entire Bible because it had already been embraced as Divinely inspired and the infallible word of God. Religion had gone too far projecting the perfection portrayal of their scriptures and found them selves backed into a corner. To change the exodus event now would destroy their Biblical credibility and diminish the church's power of control. This would leave too many pews empty on the Sabbath. Thus it is, that the most profound Biblical book gathers dust on a shelf. It is interesting to note that----

1. – There is no account of ten plagues in the Book of Jasher. There was nothing of a plague nature that forced the Pharaoh to allow

the Israelites to leave Egypt and only fear of a huge rebellion would appear to be the deciding factor.

2. – A deal was made to pay the Israelites so much for most of their livestock other then breeding pairs because excess numbers would not survive the transit through the desert. It looked like an amiable business deal but after the Israelites had left, it was discovered that Egypt had paid for more than what was received. Even back in those days, the Israelites appeared to be a very enterprising race. The enraged Pharaoh then sent his army in chase to claim what retribution he had in mind.

3. – **The book of Jasher relates that there was a narrow sand bar in the lake that was crossed during the night. Water on both sides made it seem that the sea had separated, so imaginations produced a miracle of God splitting the sea.**

Though similar conditions were not noticed to prevail later, it does not exclude it as natural situation. Those acquainted with the power of wind, and water currents know that underwater dunes can shift more quickly than on land and shipwrecks, for example, have been exposed one day and then covered over completely the next.

4. – **Jasher states that the army of Egypt never attempted to cross the sea but later scribes livened up the story and drowned the entire Egyptian army. If this had actually been so, enemy countries would surely have invaded Egypt soon after but there is no record of this ever happening.**

5. – **From Jasher, we know that Moses was in close touch at the time with his father-in-law Jethro, a Midianite priest and son of Essau and it is quite possible that the Ten Commandments were given to him by Jethro. No mention of braking the tablets was made by Jasher but he did verify that Moses had his police force of the tribe of Levi slay Nadab and Abihu along with over 3000 men from their camp. The real reason**

for this killing was far different than the one conveyed in the Bible that these people were worshipping a false God. According to Jasher, these men were with Moses at a secret meeting on the mountain and defied Moses's instructions to tell their people that they witnessed a conversation Moses had with the Lord and was told what to do.

6. – Also mentioned in Jasher's book was the war campaign against the Moabites, Midianites and Amorites where all the men, women and children were slain except the virgins. These were brought back into camp and defiled by the elders and other Israelites. Much later Moses decided that all the children born of these women were against God's will, so he had all of them and their children slain and when the slaughter ceased, some twenty four thousand women and children had been killed. After Moses died, the Israelites continued with this same genocide when they later defeated the other tribes in the land of Canaan, killing all but the virgins. Can anyone guess what respect the Bible would have if the Book of Jasher was included in its proper place?.

There is little need to go further; the book must be read to get the full impact of the actions during that period. It's no wonder the book of Jasher was excluded from the Bible. This Jasher documented knowledge would have deemed Moses insane and exposed the Israelites lust for killing along with their fetish for virgins.

7. - Accounts of other incidents before his time, was given to Jasher by his father Caleb, grandfather Hezron and his mother Azuba. The book told about Noah building a ship for fishing purposes but a flood was never mentioned. Observing other people survive famines with food from the sea, it's logical that some Israelite would copy this procedure. Under

these circumstances, is it possible that Noah may have been the first commercial fisherman in his day?

8. - The Israelites never trusted Moses for he was raised as an Egyptian and his sister Miriam was their real leader until her death while the tribe was still in the desert.

There are many questionable things about the forty years spent in the desert, also. Water is important for existence in a desert and usually found at an oasis.

Now some curious heretic might ask, "In what desert is there a single oasis large enough to support two million people and their animals?"

Many occurrences in the desert were given supernatural views of a Divine intervention and Moses related that God said this or did that so he could control his people. What had often been normal desert events now became miracles performed by Jehovah.

The manna sent from heaven is a natural interaction between lice and the oasis trees when a sweet sap surfaces, crystallizes, blows loose by the wind and scatters over the ground. But this couldn't feed some two million people for if an oasis had that many trees, it would no longer be a desert. The quail story is another projected miracle by Jehovah to feed his people.

Actually, birds migrate to and fro with the seasons in many parts of the world and crossing a desert would naturally be more difficult. They must make stops for water and if the source is dried up or contaminated with bacteria such as West Nile virus, the birds could weaken and fall to the ground while crossing the desert.

This sounds logical, for many Israelites who ate the birds became sick and died. If birds with this virus were eaten without being cooked thoroughly, this could easily happen. Wood isn't abundant in a desert for cooking so this condition wouldn't be surprising. If there was no other way of preserving the meat and rather then have it spoil or thrown away, it made sense to eat as much as possible. Moses praised the Lord for providing them with this food but couldn't figure why they were getting sick and dying by the thousands. So to get God off the hook for giving them foul fowl, Moses said God put a curse on them for being such gluttons. The question is, "What kind of God would be so harsh on anyone for having a second helping of quail?"

When examined carefully we will find exaggerations and errors in the Bible that fits neither history nor logic. Many stories can be traced to copy earlier events of other cultures that held the Israelites captive for a period of time. We should not try to solve modern troubles with words of ancient writers who still believed in a flat world, and whose 'attics' were still filled with the cobwebs of superstitions passed on from pagan ancestors. Also, adhering to mythical fears designed for mind control has left billions of minds incapable of sane reasoning and restricting civil progress. Religions take advantage of the fears they have created and then offer illusionary security to fearful people if they join them. Some may ask if it is right to destroy their false security and on the surface this would appear to be a hard question. However, if this would stop the insane killing, suffering and destruction in wars that religions condone, the answer would be a qualified, yes.

for anther chapter -

There is nothing so devastating as wars. The poor and middle class will bear the greatest burden and sacrifice the most while predators at the top will sit back and make huge profits from the war. Like animals they have no conscience but should be treated with smaller respect because animals only kill when they must have food to survive. The appetite of human predators, however, desire accumulating up to a million or billion times what it takes to exist comfortably at the expense of the suffering of others, the environment, our country, etc. Their egos and minds are so scarred over that they no longer experience shame. Pity them, for they must walk in shoes of the downtrodden in their next lifetime to become aware of the mistakes they have created in the past. No one shall escape the law of cause and effect.

Look at the loss of lives, countless cripples, orphaned children, plus disease and suffering that spreads after the devastation of properties. Also, there is destruction of fabulous cities and the cultural offerings of a beautiful people that reside therein. Are we so selfish and indulged with our egos that no rationale persists? Have we not yet discovered why we are here? Can we not realize that no war is ever won if either side has lost a son?

Cause of Our Biggest Problem

(Wars poverty, etc are only problem effects let us face reality and talk about the cause)

Though it may not register with us at first, that the biggest problem we now face is not wars, poverty, pollution, etc. As was stated in many chapters before, the whole universe relies on its main law of cause and effect. All the negative things large and small that we are experiencing now in our daily lives are the end results or effects and our first blame for its causes are usually heaped upon other people. There are also the excuses given for erroneous mistakes in circumstances surrounding those closer to us or it may be something more personal.

Most of these liable things are stressed on minor or superficial effects but somewhere down the line there has to be base accountability that has nothing to do with Satan as the culprit. Let us stop passing the buck on those we consider responsible for these woes or all those imaginable sins that run counter to our sanctimonious concepts. These so called effects that we feel to be negative and consider them problems are because most of us have yet to realize; that all things progress in a perfect manner. The universal law of cause and effect still functions at 100%. Perhaps not to our liking, but then again why should it be? The difficulty here is that a majority of us have not the faintest idea what is actually going on.

Primary actions may be singular or in mass and they produce causes which in turn promotes an effect. We can be responsible for making our life and environment more peaceful resembling a little bit of heaven but if too many mistakes are made it could be more like a hell on earth. The power is ours to make society what we want it to be. With this process, however, negative mistakes must be avoided or it will never be. This means we have to get over our egotism that we are the 'spoon that stirs the coffee' and know what is best for everybody if done our way. To be successful we cannot ignore freedoms, equalities or tolerance.

Those living in an illusionary world of security whose songs like 'Leaning on His everlasting Arms' have a twisted idea of their liability. Responsibility is not praying for something to happen or be given us but rather to gather needed knowledge and apply it to the problem 'at hand.'

Is not this, why we are here, to learn and grow? Let us say for instance, that the 'Master Mind' projects a lesson for an immediate experience. Are we going to refute the knowledge of an 'All Knowing Source,' on what is best for us? It is amazing how the blind follow the blind and human ignorance has been 'carbon copied' for some two thousand years.

We can surmise how ancient concepts were passed on to our illiterate forbearers for countless years, but to be accepted without verifiable proof by us living in highly educated systems, signifies how much the brain's right hemisphere has been neglected. Relying too heavily on data that is stored in our memory banks is a mistake, for not only is it programmed with countless human errors of our time but also of misjudgments that takes us back thousands of years. If the right half of our brain has not rescued us with relative thinking by now, are we then deemed halfwits?

Manipulations of religious threats and fears have held civilization back with radical notions and sanctimonious rules to obey. So long as traditional dogma is followed, we are in trouble for many years to come. Some argue that if it were not for religion, humans would not know right from wrong. This statement is nothing more than ignorant rhetoric and unthinking people do not realize they are insulting a higher power with such remarks. Are we inferring that this power was stupid because a conscience was omitted with the creation of our species? Would this not be impossible when this power is all knowing? Should we agree that this Divine power made souls, then what is our point? Our conscience must have surely come with the 'wall paper' as it were.

Erroneous religious concepts are the major cause of human misery, large and small. This will be clearly illustrated later on in this chapter.

We must not be discouraged to the point of stress for our personal errors. All of us have a weakness for lack of knowledge at times but is part of our ongoing experiences. This only becomes a sticky problem when our egos get ruffled and refuses to back off. Much time and effort is then spent trying to defend our 'radical drift ' for perhaps a better part of life. How very sad, to let vanity in control of our thinking. Is such an attitude really worth it?

The most catastrophic condition we must eventually face and one that is likely to be ignored until too late is a population explosion. There is a reason so few want to talk about it or take on the initiative of finding a solution. From aspects relating to the situation there is a dreaded fear among congressmen of a negative backlash that hangs over them like an ominous black cloud. They are afraid to tell the truth and push for sane measures of birth control because it may mean a lack of political support from their religious constituents.

What would be considered a valid reason by religion to oppose any birth control is that some biblical writer, who never made it around the block and seldom strayed far from home for fear of falling off the edge of his flat world, mentioned that the Lord spoke to him with a message about going to the ends of the earth and multiply. Is it not rather strange that all these profound messages were repeated some two thousand years ago and whoever did the talking then must have died because the voice was never heard from again?

We might wonder that as the world became overpopulated and the people began starving why the voice did not come back to say no, no more, it was a big mistake? Has anyone ever noticed that when these voice orders go wrong, how many alibis and excuses pop up in defense of them? Most of the explanations appear to be rhetoric or mythical and all the answers seem to produce more questions than there were before.

First we must be honest and list most negative things that happen when a country is over populated. Some of it may have a bigger impact in one area than another but an overall effect can be disastrous to healthy self-supporting societies. Some of the negative applications are…

1. – Over population creates poverty by allowing more people than the land or country can support. When this becomes acute, starvation or malnutrition is apt to ensue.   If this generates into a common situation, then trying to help by providing food for the starving millions will only make matters worse in future years if there are no birth control measures in place. Take East India for example, the birth rate might multiply ten times with each generation and if one million were saved from starving, then a situation is now created where ten million might be starving.

2. – Over population means more pollution and stress on existing municipalities and if not taken care of properly would induce disease and in a case of chemical waste it can produce premature

deaths or that of severe handicaps for a lifetime. This would also put additional burdens on our healthcare and welfare systems.

3. – Over population can wreck havoc with our educational systems, for lack of tax dollars, by cutting out art, music, sports and activities that make the system interesting enough to help children graduate from high school and keep them from 'falling through the cracks' as it were. It is unaffordable for most middle wage earners to now send their children to college, for better paying jobs are being downsized and companies are having their work shipped overseas even supporting communist nations instead of preserving democracy. 'Pinko communists' once labeled on liberals now rests firmly on conservative shoulders. College degrees no longer carry with it a promising future, for engineering along with other professions are already being steered to foreign countries. If average citizens have not figured out who the real traitors of our country are by now, then they will continue to suffer for errors made at voting booths. .

4. – Over population creates breeding grounds for crimes of all sorts.

What happens when people are denied their skilled jobs, are about to lose their homes, cars and possibly other security measures like health care that they can no longer afford. The land of opportunity is fading fast and we are no longer a united people dedicated to make this country strong and respectful to all its citizens. Bigotry and prejudice are still 'bugs in our bonnets' that have made a permanent home with many.

Many of the younger generations are used to better living and are apt to turn to all sorts of crime to maintain their life styles. The stress would be even more devastating to young married couples struggling to raise a family. If they lose faith in their country, this would be the beginning of the end for us as a strong and respectable nation.

This does not look good for our country because the poorer we get, the more crime we can expect. Robbery of banks, stores, homes, along with personal attacks in parking lots or walking alone most anywhere. We must not forget also that robbery promotes more people being killed to cover getaways, identities, etc. Is this not a shame that in the future we will have little time to worry about terrorists, because we will be too busy protecting ourselves against other Americans? There would be a need to double our police force but their budgets have already been cut so the money saved can be diverted to finance presidential wars. Tax dollars needed for the increase in services due to illegal immigration is given to the rich as an excuse that it will be used to create the good jobs that were lost. This type of rhetoric has not worked in the past or ever will in the future. 'Don't eat that stuff, Elmer, them's road apples.'

Let us put our right brain hemisphere in a functional mode and seek true answers that are covered up by most of the media. If the German propaganda minister, Gobles, of WWII were to view the garbage put out by most of our news media today, he would consider himself a mere boy scout in his profession.

Would conditions be different in the world had not religions condemned the use of birth control measures because of their illusionary concepts? Are they indirectly if not directly responsible for the negative situations that were previously mentioned?

Most things in nature have a function that is positively reciprocal and if this balance is upset then it can produce a severe chain reaction that is negative. Depending on specifics everything suffers to a degree from any malfunction. Humans have acquired the intelligence to control many of the conditions about them if used in the proper manner. Control also engenders the need for established limitations to become a civilized people that recognize obligations and responsibilities. Physical survival depends on the health of our environment and anything that threatens it must be controlled. Zealots keep worrying about a mythical heavenly home and fail to realize our first obligation is to the environmental home into which we were born. A good example is the global warming issue that for many years was ignored by corrupted politicians, who could not see beyond their 'oily wallets,' even though warned decades ago by our scientists of what would happen if the needs for a balanced environment were not met. Population is in the same dangerous situation where the worldwide food shortages and fresh water supplies will not be able to keep up with population growth. Even in this country, just a few natural disasters would be enough to create a chaotic condition across the entire country. Earth is home and much too precious to ignore its well being, 'as mother nature goes, so shall we.' We cannot take everything from the earth's resources and give nothing back. To reaffirm this, it would be best talking to a smart farmer. He too would not raise more animals than his land could support.

Another weakness we have is an urge to be perfect and are tempted to believe that it is the ultimate goal of superiority, when in reality the feedback can hang like an 'albatross' of bad luck around our necks..

From an operational point of view, perfection is a non-sequester or an impossible function for a human to attain. Yet, religion would have us believe they have perfect answers to our problems but when maneuvered into a corner, they cannot blame God, who is in control, of course, so they invented Satan to 'take the rap' and keep the monkey off of God's back. Then when sensible questions cannot be answered we are apt to hear a 'have faith' gimmick which is another psychological 'sugar pill.' But what about all of the marriages that are made in heaven, then who is to blame for over half of the church weddings that end in divorce?

A common drawback is that millions have never studied or reviewed other religions and the tainted presumptions of them are received through family hearsay or the prejudiced opinions of their own clergy.

How then can we possibly relate to the world around us and make a personal decision of what is best for our family, community or country, if we allow ourselves to be swayed by religious concepts, political bias and then fall victims of a status quo that cater only to a select few?

We have become so absorbed with our personal lives, good times, etc. and ignored the basic ingredients in life that would make such a big difference for our families and future generations. The things that have happened here in recent years would not likely be tolerated in Europe for these people take an avid interest in politics and demand credibility from those in government positions.

When we started buying autos, big equipment and large appliances from foreign countries instead of supporting our veterans who worked in these factories to make a living, it was the beginning of a sad end. The hypocrites now try to cover up their selfish mistakes with signs reading, 'Support our Troops.' What irony when there are no good jobs to come home to and service suicides almost double each year. A most important thing we Americans seem to have lost is our conscience, which is easily demonstrated by the number of foreign car owners passing by.

PSYCHOLOGY

(Freud also practiced hypnotism on his more difficult cases but at what depth it was used is a moot question)

Over many centuries, great philosophers have laid the groundwork for our later efforts in modern psychology. Like medicine for the physical, the treatment of our mental side was also a slow process of what made us 'tick' and what 'ticked us off.' In the early 20th century it was thought that inherited intelligence was responsible for human actions and a study of phrenology (skull bumps) became an art form. This practice was soon 'bumped' when more thought was given to brain size and weight but this was 'dumped' also when it was discovered that Einstein's brain flunked most of these standards.

A psychologist named, Sigmund Freud, finally entered the 'picture' with a new theory and his systematic approach made more sense and was generally adopted by others in his field. It was considered a great step forward in the further exploration of psychiatry. Until that time, formed opinions were randomly based on individual conclusions.

Contributions that Freud made concerning the ego were important but were derived solely from objective perspectives and influenced decisions accordingly. Freud was also adamant in supporting his rigid concept of hormones and sex to the point where one might get the impression that his eyelids were made of foreskins. One thing he tried before the others became involved was a limited practice of hypnotism that was successful in many of his cases but to what depth it was used is a moot question.

Not long after most of Freud's ideas were generally accepted, Alfred Adler appeared on the scene and added more complex adjustments of a subtle nature to the art. Adler's ideas had no immediate impact in the beginning for he spent more time refining than promoting his concepts.

This later changed, however, and he became the first psychologist to conduct group therapy classes using his principles.

It was not long before Jung, Stern, and other respected men in this field began to practice views similar to those of Adler, but experience that he gained as a medic during WW1 gave him a definite edge over his counterparts. Although, Freud shifted psychology from 'low drive' to a 'higher drive' 'per se,' it was Alfred Adler who was most responsible for taking the profession to a still higher level that has become a norm from which modern versions now operate.

When hypnosis becomes more acceptable and extended to include past lives, it will take psychology to a much higher level than ever before and have a significant impact on curing patients. This, plus improving a general awareness at the public level would enhance an understanding of our purpose in life that was not realized before.

Adler believed that when striving to better human society, it should not be evaluated from political or religious viewpoints but rather from the accumulated data of scientific research. That life of a human soul is not only our awareness thereof, but also the growing factor of it to be. This is akin to Plato's philosophy that the consciousness of truth is ever becoming.

Adler stated, "Our moral purpose must logically be, that of uniting the individuals into a society where the greatest aspects of the human race are aptly safeguarded."

This concept is sadly neglected in today's society, however, where class predators under the guise of freedom are robbing and polluting our resources along with using the world's inhabitants as human equations to satiate their greed. They appear to have no conscience and their actions duplicate those of immoral animals.

By making life poorer for the average American, its pushes mothers out the door for added income to help the family survive. To do this she must leave preschoolers in others care.

This makes it more difficult for sustaining family values and the most affected are the small children. They lack the loving care and parental guidance so necessary at that stage in their lives. Most young minds have already established attitudes and have adapted to life lifestyles by the time they are four or five years old. When the future realities do not coincide with already formed views, confusion is the usual result. This restricts personal capabilities and the progressive action that contributes to a more civil and healthy society. There are many things to discover about the human mind and what influences us to think as we do. Sadly, there are no knobs to switch mind channels when they are needed most.

A person must learn to think relatively and read between the lines, as it were, to receive a more accurate intuitive picture. This is most difficult to do with all the distractions in everyday living Modern conveniences would also be included where most thinking is done for us with little or no effort involved. We rarely have to exercise our brain with visualizing what we read anymore because it is already pictured for us.

Even the words to music are acted out on videocassettes. To top this, loud repeating drumbeats drown out finer music of higher vibrations that cannot be appreciated later in life because our eardrums are scarred over by then.

As hypnotism reveals more evidence of reincarnation, which is based on a natural law of cause and effect, and the proof of past lives becomes overwhelming it will have to be universally accepted. Hypnotism has the power to unlock karmic knowledge that has an immense bearing on the healing effort of those with psychosomatic conditions. Considering consistency in averages of published results by reputable professionals in their field during the last fifty years, it is safe to assume that thousands of cases and instances can relate to the validity of reincarnation.

The 20th century prophet, Edgar Cayce, diagnosed illnesses and the treatment thereof that cured hundreds of people who had come to him for help. He did all this from a self induced sleep and remembered nothing of it when he awoke so all that was said had to be copied and recorded for accuracy. The knowledge of past lives and personal karma was used to correct problems of those afflicted with otherwise hidden ailments.

Follow up research of family background or historical data usually confirmed the validity of his readings unless it was far back in time and too difficult to trace.

All told, Cayce gave over two thousand such readings. It is easy for those of intelligence who have studied the principles of reincarnation to discover several places in the Christian Bible where the action thereof is irrefutable, although it is not mentioned by name. In two places Jesus and his disciples were involved in discussions about it and the related outcome was a glaring fact that they believed in reincarnation.

The problem is that most religionist never studied the principals of cause and effect of which reincarnation is a perfect example. Many will relate to an ignorant version of transmigration using animals, birds, etc., and from this believe it to be the same thing. The reluctance to research this law of cause and effect stems from our fear of the unknown and the human resistance to change.

We can easily prove all of this for ourselves by getting the 'boogie man' off our backs and hire a professional hypnotist who can regress us to another lifetime. For proof or security, all this can then be done in the presence of relatives or friends and recorded on tape so the information not too far back can be checked out and re-affirmed.

Why are we afraid to open another 'door,' is it fear of the truth?

Reincarnation is not a religion or cult, but a personal realization by research, meditation, psychic impressions and hypnotism.

Furthermore it is not limited to normal boundaries or rules nor is it proxy to any one organized institution.

We must always respect the added information that wise men have to offer us but never to the point of idolizing them. It becomes a danger should their ideas become stereotyped as a panacea or ultimate answer and advancement beyond that point is apt to be ignored or silenced.

It must be realized that what the wise have exposed is just one step of many to follow but this is often overlooked by some inventors and even those most of us consider to be a genius. If not an ego problem, it could be that they were over focused on their own brainchild and stopped wondering what was behind the other 'door.'

Looking back through history, one of these two reasons appears to have held back still greater things from these very accomplished men. Let us take a brief look.

Freud gave great contributions to his field of psychology and that of psychiatry but he did not research the subjective aspects of his profession thoroughly as did Adler. Now, a man of Freud's intelligence must have recognized more complex things surrounding his initial findings but he overlooked the significance that they deserved.

One of Thomas Edison's many inventions was an electrical system that used a direct current. Shortly thereafter, Nikola Tesla, came along with the alternating current system that was far superior for long distance transmission of electricity but Edison's ego fought against it for years. It was a losing battle because industry quickly recognized its advantages and adopted Tesla's alternating current.

Brilliant as Albert Einstein was, for some reason he could not bring himself to believe in the Quantum Theory even when presented to him by his peers. All during his life, Einstein did not accept nor sanction the Quantum Theory

One of our greatest minds today, Stephan Hawking, was given the highest honor of the scientific community when an Isaac Newton Award was bestowed upon him for his work on a new physics concept. Later, however, he presented proof that his first calculations were wrong.

This is quite rare and goes to show that there are endless anomalies to be considered. It may be mere conjecture but, Hawking, having lived a good part of his life in a wheelchair, it would be no chore to humble the ego and press on for further information and answers. To whit, where would we be in computer science today, if Gates and others were to conceive that the first software was perfect?

These examples prove wisdom as a progressive act of consciousness.

It also appears to be logically limitless in every sense of the word and if this is true than it is also eternal and cannot be otherwise.

Isn't it time for our own sake and that of future generations to stop blaming others for the plight that was created in our world? To sit back and do nothing in the belief that God is in control is a no-brainer. We were born with a free will and are responsible for creating our society either directly or indirectly, during the time span we are here. Literally speaking, why do we spend half of our time under a table hiding from a make believe Satan and the other half praying to an Old Testament God, who sanctioned genocide and the stoning to death of others? If we are to believe in the Bible and the warnings it gives us about the Antichrists, then we should begin thinking about what it means. An Antichrist would be one who opposed what Jesus stood for and all the positive things that were taught. An Antichrist would be one who was anti-brotherhood, anti- love, anti-tolerance, anti-peace, anti-concern for lives of others who don't have the same mind set as their own, etc. Off hand, the Christian Bible seems to judge and condemn Ann Coulter and Pat Robertson as the two biggest Antichrists of our time.

Are we still buying her hate books and supporting a preacher who condones assassinations?

When dealing with psychology issues we cannot believe everything told us nor trust the actions of others for the warnings are clear that there are many 'wolves in sheep's clothing' that prey on the naïve for personal gain and/or power. It is difficult for the weak minded to grasp a situation for they habitually follow the crowd for security in numbers and have not bothered using the other portion of their brain to a deductive advantage.

Charlatans in the religious and political fields know they can control us by creating confusion with falsely pretending a non-existent situation that would challenge our illusionary comfort zone. In one of many ways they play upon our fears and the bigotry we have of other people.

Under these conditions, good reasoning must be used to counteract such influence with a more positive stance. This would eliminate those backlashes, which would be sure to follow, were we to follow the crowd and strengthen their propaganda agendas.

The reluctance to change is because we are convinced that what was taught us is correct and the truth. Yet, we ignore the fact that this is an illusion, for any improvement entails change. Everything is in constant flux both macrocosms and microcosms and change is a natural law of the universe. We are a growing element along with it, which also includes our minds as well as bodies.

Let us not be confused with befuddled descriptions of reality and actuality. They are often used reflecting the same meaning. Reality is the 'twin sister' of realization and this is a personal attribute and can differ with each person's outlook. Actuality is unyielding, a supreme factor of what is, an unchangeable 'iron' manifestation of the moment and like a complete truth, is out of the domain of human realization.

Another dilemma we face is that a majority of American children are trained to be dependent upon others whose decisions rely on predetermined thought originated from superstitious minds of pagan ancestors thousands of years ago. Most young minds have already established attitudes and adapted life styles by the time they are four or five years old. When future realities do not coincide with already formed views, confusion is the usual result. This restricts personal capabilities and the progressive action that contributes to a more civil and healthy society. There are many things yet to be discovered about the human mind and what influences us to think as we do? Sadly, we cannot turn knobs to switch mind channels when needed. A person must learn to think relatively and read between the lines intuitively and this is most difficult with all the distractions in our everyday lives. These would include many modern conveniences where most of our thinking including some manual chores is done for us with little or no effort involved. We don't have to exercise our brain by visualizing what is read anymore because much of it is pictured and even the words to music are acted out in videocassettes. To top this, loud repeating drumbeats drown out finer music of higher vibrations that can't be appreciated later in life because the eardrums are scarred over.

As hypnotism reveals more evidence of reincarnation, which is based on natural law of cause and effect, it will become scientifically acceptable, for it produces karmic knowledge that can have an immense healing effect with psychosomatic conditions.

Considering consistency in the averages of published results by reputable doctors and psychiatrists during the last fifty years, it is safe to assume that thousands of cases and instances can relate to the validity of reincarnation.

Contributions that Freud made concerning the ego were important but derived only from objective perspectives and his decisions were made accordingly. Although responsible for much progress in psychiatry, Freud was adamant in supporting his rigid concept relating to hormones and sex. At times, one might get the impression that certain of his views were generated by eyelids made of foreskins. Not long after most of Freud's ideas were generally accepted, Alfred Adler appeared on the scene and added more complex adjustments of a subtle nature to the art. Adler's ideas had no immediate impact on the profession in the beginning for he spent more time and effort refining his concepts than promoting them. This later changed and he became the first psychologist to conduct group therapy classes using his principles. In the early twentieth century, Jung, Stern, and other men respected in this field, also began to practice views similar to those used by Adler, but the expertise gained as a doctor during WWI, gave him a significant edge over the others. Freud shifted psychology from low gear into second, as it were, but Alfred Adler was most responsible for taking it to a higher level that has become the norm from which the modern profession now operates. When hypnosis became popular and was used more frequently as a tool, it boosted the potential of psychiatry into a comparative overdrive. Adler believed that when striving to better human society, it should not be evaluated from political or religious viewpoints but rather from the accumulated data of scientific research.

Einstein, as brilliant as he was, could not bring himself to believe in the Quantum Theory when presented to him by other scientists.

Extra info. – do not print

For security reasons we want to know more about the mysteries of life, however, there may be good reason for further enlightenment to remain dormant until it is earned. Does greed, bigotry, disregard of our environment and support of wars signify that we are worthy and prepared to handle a greater wisdom?

Freud gave us significant contributions in his field but didn't research the subjective aspects thoroughly as did Adler. He must have been aware of some but obviously didn't give them much priority.

impressions to e that his eyelids were made kof foreshims)

Isn't it time for our own sake and that of future generations to face the truth and give the planet's inhabitants another chance to redeem themselves?

Let us touch on just one more thing before we move on and that is the danger of harboring fear. Most of us with a belief in religion were raised in fear and this is the evilest of crimes perpetrated on the human mind, whether deliberate or not. It cripples the mind and shuts the door on freedom of thought. It is a tool of control and stifles even our ability to love unconditionally. We then roam around in a confused state and often wonder why we can't find true happiness. If we cannot successfully overcome our fears, then it is time to seek professional help but steer clear of the religious kind, for the chances are that most problems began from this bigoted source. How, can it be otherwise, when religions teach a prejudice that theirs is right and all others are false? Such attitudes promote distrust, resentment, hate and eventual violent confrontations.

One of our greatest minds of today, Stephan Hawking, was given the highest honor of the scientific community when an Isaac Newton Award was bestowed upon him for his work on a new physics concept. Sometime later, however, he presented proof that his calculations were wrong. This is quite rare but goes to show that there are endless anomalies yet to be considered. It may be mere conjecture but, Hawking, having lived a good part of life in a wheelchair, it would be no chore for him to humble his ego and press on for further information and answers. To wit, where would we be in computer science today, if Gates and others were to conceive that his first software was perfect?

One of Thomas Edison's many inventions was an electrical direct current system.

Over many centuries, great philosophers have laid the groundwork for our later efforts in modern psychology. Like medicine treating the physical, the treatment of our mental side was also a slow process of what made us 'tick' and what 'ticked us off'! In the 19th century they thought inherited intelligence was responsible for human actions and the study of phrenology (skull bumps) became an art form. This practice was 'bumped' in the next century and more thought was given to brain size and weight but this concept was later 'dumped' in the 20th century, when Einstein's brain flunked this criterion. Earlier in the century, Freud entered the picture with his new theory and this systematic approach made more sense and was generally adopted by others in his field as a great step toward the further exploration of psychiatry. Until then, formed opinions in the profession were randomly based on individual conclusions.

Psychology

Reincarnation is not a religion or cult but a personal realization through research, meditation, psychic impressions and hypnotism. Furthermore it's not limited to normal boundaries or rules nor is it proxy to any one organized institution.

Shortly thereafter Tesla came along with an alternating current system that was far better for long distance transfer of electricity but Edison's ego fought against it for years even though it was so obviously superior that it was quickly adopted by industry for general public use.

Start and end the day positively, remember that a friendly smile casts no shadows.

That life of a human soul is not merely the realization thereof, but a growing factor to be. This is akin to Plato's philosophy that consciousness of truth is ever becoming. Adler stated that our moral purpose must logically be of uniting individuals into a society where the greatest aspects of the human race are aptly safeguarded. This concept is sadly neglected in today's society, however, where class division predators are robbing our resources under the guise of freedom and using the world's inhabitants as human equations to satisfy their greed. They appear to have no conscience and their actions duplicate those of immoral animals.

The 20th century prophet, Edgar Cayce was instrumental in scores of recorded cases, where knowledge of personal karma was used to correct health problems of those afflicted with hidden disorders. Follow up research of historical data and family records have repeatedly confirmed the validity of reincarnation. References in the Christian Bible appear to confirm that Jesus and his disciples also believed in this principle. This is far more accurate and credible than blind belief in unproven hearsay that was handed down for generations by some ancient writers with inaccurate opinions of our world and many other things. Most religious zealots never studied the principles of reincarnation and attempt to deride it with an ignorant version of transmigration with the use of animals, etc. The reluctance to research this universal law stems from a common human resistance for change and fear of the unknown. People can prove all of this for themselves if they can get the 'boogey man' off their backs and have a professional hypnotist regress them to another lifetime; all in the presence of relatives or friends and recorded on tape so information not too far back can be checked out and re-affirmed. If we are 'chicken' to do this, then we shouldn't 'knock it'.

These examples prove to us that wisdom is a growing element of our consciousness and shouldn't stop with just one discovery. Consciousness is then logically limitless in every sense of the word and if this is true than it is also eternal. It cannot be otherwise.

Total freedom is a myth for we are all dependent on each other in some way, shape or form. Democracy is a form of government where we must function psychically and physically as a family in order to support one another. Big egos are in bigger trouble then they can imagine if they ignore this fact. When we can no longer live, one for all and all for one in a reciprocal fashion, then we have lost the chance of becoming civilized beings. Does anyone of a right mind think that we are living up to this test with all the wars and suffering that we have created? When we deviate from moral unity the gap widens and corruption seeps in, which in turn will foster greed, hate and distrust in one another. These same actions, many times over have destroyed past civilizations but our 'all knowing ignorance' fails to learn from this lesson.

We must recognize the fact that we will never have a perfect world but the lessons to experience don't have to be wars, forced poverty, eliminating family security and that of destroying a healthy environment for the sake of a privileged few. It is insane to imagine that our Creator would approve of immoral predators robbing earthly resources and subjecting human resources to an animal status as well, to satiate personal greed, glorification and wield unjust power over others. It is not surprising to see these actions supported by bigoted religions and brings the curtain down to expose them for what they really stand for. s used and also collaborated with the right hemisphere. Are we, for the most part, only memorizing the logic of others stored in the left memory bank without using reason syllogistically? How can any degrees of logic be determined if we cannot think in a relative manner? Reality is a creation of the mind whereas actuality is the pure truth of what is and the human mind is yet incapable of understanding the latter, for we are still evolving and perhaps on a lower rung of the ladder to boot.

We should always respect the added information that wise men have to offer but never to the point of idolizing them for then their ideas are usually stereotyped as a panacea or the ultimate answer and advancement beyond that point is apt to be ignored or silenced. It should be realized that what the wise have exposed is just one step of many to follow, however, this point is easily overlooked by some inventors and even those considered a genius. This may be the result of ego problems or being so focused on improving their brainchild that they have stopped wondering what is behind the other door. Looking back through history it has happened to many accomplished men in their eras. Let us take a look at the work of these few wise men a moment -

FORGIVENESS AND LOVE

(What is true about forgiveness? If forgiving is for an assumed wrong
how was the judgment made and was it a sole opinion?)

Is forgiveness an act of love? At first glance we are apt to agree
with a general consensus that it is. The question is why? An honorable
thought that's applied to the word forgiveness doesn't necessarily mean
that the emotion of love is the root cause. Like many combinations in
languages, much is taken out of context in an attempt to fortify some
concept. This is especially so when used for propaganda purposes.
Negative intent is usually glossed over with an attachment of words
that already have a symbolic meaning of high respect.

To find what affinity forgiveness has with love we must put it
under an analyzing scope using relative deductions. This then reveals
ugly mini-creatures clinging to the word that makes its affiliation
with love seem even more remote.

Our first impression of the word 'forgiveness' suggests it to be
the honorable act of a good deed. Holy books stress forgiveness as
an act of compassion and the right thing to do. As with all thought,
however, conceptions derived from human minds are prone to error.
Primarily, we assume this righteous attitude to be true but in all
probability there is an induced feeling of superiority over supposed
wrongdoers. Then too, the premise of a gracious overture may be

made for imagined rewards of Divine favor. The act of forgiveness in such a case would be for selfish ends thereby negating its purpose. Some infer that forgiveness entails a positive action of compassion and therefore becomes an attribute of love. This again is taken out of context and relative questions must be asked in search of a more truthful response.

What are the true circumstances behind the words, " I forgive"

Are we not actually saying, " I forgive your wrong doing?"

In this light, such statements are then subject for review and query.

How and who validated the action as a wrong?

Did both parties have a say in the decision?

If something was wrong according to a particular code, what caused it?

Was an act by the forgiver, such as lack of patience, sensitivity, etc, responsible for the breakdown that incited a negative reaction?

What was the physical and/or mental condition of the accused when the incident in question occurred?

Did the forgiver try walking in the 'moccasins' of the other person before making such a judgment?

Was a forgiver's attitude a guilt transfer of some personal error that was committed in their past?

Lest we succumb to illusionary traps; is it not better for us to first rationalize a situation?

To challenge the authenticity of anything is not only our right but also a must for the ascent to a higher level of awareness.

There are concepts that place importance on subconscious behavior while some relate to the karmic action of cause and effect. Still others may adhere to any variety of theological beliefs. Because of this reason, descriptions here will attempt to cover varied thought in a constructive manner and though some words or expressions used here may seem out of place or slightly foreign to some, they are not meant to be derogatory to any principle. 'There are many roads that lead to Rome' and the more knowledge we survey makes us better equipped to deal with adversity. What may be perceived as doubtful, including this material, should be subjectively analyzed so the clarity of import can be fully realized. Pertaining to this, we often hear a phrase 'let's sleep on it first.' This allows time for data to be processed by the 'soul internet' so that a much clearer picture can be projected on our screen of objective perception. By delving into the mysteries of life, that we are free to do, there will be many factors to consider. The cosmic (all pervading universal force) positions us for lessons in numerous ways.

We become angry and upset when something is not easily understood or difficult for our ego to accept. Candid examples or demonstrations are then often needed to clarify our circumstances and afford the opportunity to improve what may be corrected. From this perspective then, instead of posturing ourselves in a forgiving mode, we can take a position of humble gratitude for these cosmic lessons that are given us. When our attitude functions in this manner, presumed wrongs become temporary inconveniences. What at first appears to be a negative condition would then be turned into a positive situation. This example illustrates the alchemical formula for mutating base ingredients and transforming them into an exalted state. This functions on both exoteric and esoteric levels.

After experiencing the ill affects of negative activity our self, we should be sensitive to what others may be going through and allow a compassionate attitude toward them. To recognize and accept the need for our own forgiveness then reduces an assumed reason to forgive someone else. Rather then challenging cosmic teaching methods, we should be thankful for the living demonstrations portrayed each day for our benefit.

An adequate understanding of a situation is necessary before a sense of compassion is attained and this isn't possible until empathy between the parties is established. Thus accomplished it negates any recognition of forgiveness, for from that moment on, it is silently induced. As this action is intuitively reflected, it accomplishes three things, repentance, forgiveness and the automatic removal of guilt.

Dealing with the aftermath of the physically or mentally abused persons, the answers are more complex taking on other relative factors. It generally would seem right for the abused to forgive the tormentors and get on with their lives. But here again, forgiveness bears the taint of wrongdoing against and carries with it a danger of resentment and hate.

Regardless of sentiment, if this action influences their thoughts, the abused may become part of the negative action taken against them. These poor people don't need any additional burdens.

By seeing ourselves in the negativity of others we may realize the purpose of its action. Once we know our relationship with the cause, the effect can then be reconciled more quickly. Is it mere coincidence that most of the abused have guilt feelings that somehow they are responsible for violence taken against them? With hate and retaliation successfully removed, detrimental side effects would be eliminated and the abused could then experience peace and rapport with their internal counterpart.

There is an old repeated saying, "I'll forgive but I won't forget."

This is another misconception of the truth and like a 'yoyo' with another string attached its purpose becomes nullified.

Were someone to slap our face, would it be better to gratify the ego and say, "I forgive you" when in reality we should humbly say, "thank you I needed that?"

We cannot know what's under a stone unturned or the degree in truth of anything, until it is exposed to the light. Therefore, it is essential to question all hearsay whether from oral or written sources, for the gift of reason is the pathway to a higher level of consciousness and a better understanding of the truth. This will naturally gives us a mental edge to deal successfully with problems that we may face from day to day. Life will become easier and we can be enjoying more of the good life. To be recognized everything begins with the mind and thoughts are actually things with the power of positive and negative functions. Unless we are able to think beyond the normal acceptance of what is generally known, the elixir of life to stay young at heart will disappear. It is curiosity and imagination that moves us forward to greater things. Along with this we must practice tolerance, show respect and reflect our soul love towards others. Without this we are merely 'empty shells' being washed ashore.

So many times in life we look for answers to questions or problems that appear to be unsolvable. It matters little if we believe in it or not, most profound answers can logically be arrived at by using the key principles of reincarnation. The main problem concerning western culture is our adamant refusal to study seriously the views of other concepts. All kinds of proof are available but we are fearful to step beyond the threshold of accepted thought to that of the unknown. Any attempt to circumvent the immutable law of the universe (cause and effect) is presumptuous and illusionary. All of nature functions by this law and nothing can change it. To solve our problems large and small, we must continually seek for better alternatives and cultivate a closer relationship with our soul self.

In the previous chapter, some information was given about 'Edgar Cayce' books but there are numerous other books for sale about past lives including many authored by professionals. It takes an open and humble mind to search beyond the confines of superstition and myth, which have traumatized our minds by fear.

LOVE

(There is only one essence of love. Whether used to make mud pies or delicious soup, water does not alter its structure for varied results)

No word is so often used and universally respected as that denoting love. It generally expresses a selfless emotion that comes from deep within our spiritual nature. Whether this subjective impulse emanates from gross or refined states has little bearing on its prime source. That is to say, love energy does not deviate into separate values from its origin in order to produce varied results.

Sometime ago a discourse was presented in great length entertaining the idea that spiritual love possessed higher qualities in comparison with other types of love. Now, it is essential to catalogue things for ease of recall and use but in the process, relativity is often ignored. Especially evident of this is when we attempt to give a human rating to cosmic or a Creator's love.

Love is always relative to its prime source, the cosmic or Master Mind. Propagation of life and creation of all things begins with this love. Because it is observed to operate at different levels of vibratory frequencies does not alter the source. An unwitting endeavor to change any natural law of the universe is impossible. A most common weakness in judgments stem not from the basic recognition of things, but rather, in the applications thereof. For what purpose we tap into any source will determine the value that is received from it. For instance, water that is used to make mud pies or delicious chicken soup does not change its basic structure to obtain the varied results. This observation also applies to so called Divine love, which is manifested in so many ways. Values that we place on most things, take root from personal observations and biased conclusions. It then adheres to objective premises with artificial standards set by others of society and thus receives the false impressions that this love emanating from the cosmic has altered qualities.

It is true that degrees and intensities of love from various viewpoints do have valid and recognizable traits. 'No greater love is there then to lay down one's life for another' is a fairly accurate statement. Such a person would probably possess a loving selfless nature with an ego elevated to encompass others on an equal sharing base with self. The term, 'loving thy neighbor as thyself' might also apply in a similar situation. Thus, we can deduce that a foundation of true love must begin with a cornerstone of selflessness and concern for the security of others as well. These and other applications of love will not change its essence, per se. When love is used for finer purposes, it will involve an effort by those with a higher degree of awareness. The origin of love, however, remains constant, for a 'rose is a rose' etc.

Little would be gained by delving into the semantics of the word 'love' for this could run the full gamut of similar interpretations. Most of us are aware of the difficulties that would be encountered, if we tried to justify the various emotions of love. This could encompass the fringe areas with such words as like, passion, maternal love, instinct, etc. We shouldn't be overly concerned with these uses or the personal opinions thereof. It's best to let each individual develop their own pace with these balances. Rather than 'pigeon hole' anomalies of love, we can visualize it as a beautiful gift of creation manifesting in certain ways under varied conditions of reality.

The light of love is infused within us all and is the birthright from our spiritual heritage. The cosmic just is and functions under its own laws, whether we are aware of them or not. We must realize that in the natural scheme of the universe there is no east or west, no higher or lower and definitely no discrimination.

Centering love on self-satisfaction is an aspect of short duration and becomes a roadblock to its full potential. Human love that is projected with 'no strings attached' will bounce back and become reciprocal.

When love is practiced and delivered with right attitude, then we need not seek its return, for love will automatically be attracted toward us. We seldom think of love in this manner, yet, it undoubtedly can be the simplest and best used formula in the world. Difficulty in realizing this is due to social overkill on individuality and our lack of teaching the responsibility that also comes with the 'individuality package'.

We have been 'sidetracked' by most of the status quo into believing defunct myths, superstitions, and erroneous hearsay that runs counter to science, history and logical reason. Why let illusionary fears rob us of sanity and ability to think for ourselves? Religion condemns itself by teaching prejudice and bigotry, which is the opposite of love.

We are given the helm to pilot our own ship and allowing others to divert it from the 'port of love' will shipwreck us on the shoals of hate and destruction. If control cannot be maintained at the helm, then no amount of plea-bargaining for supernatural intervention will change the course. The law of cause and effect will not be denied but we are given the chance to redeem ourselves in future lives. This is a compensation law, not one of punishment. Albert Schweitzer, the famous theologian, missionary doctor and a great humanitarian (Nobel Peace Prize 1952) was asked to define our Creator and said it in three words, 'God is Love.'

We cannot expect a cosmic creator to provide us with all the answers of life, for like all else it is something to be earned and as this happens it opens doors to higher learning. Humility and meditation are conducive to this course of action for its success depends on awareness of being an integral part of all that is. When thus attuned, individuality becomes a sacrificial lamb. Are we here to develop a higher level of consciousness in preparation for chores that may be awarded us in other segments of an expanding universe? Think about it; being a microcosm of an evolving macrocosm, we can either learn and grow along with it or choose to live many less meaningful lives as observers and followers.

To know more we must have a desire to learn and to do that we must get books on diversified subjects to stimulate the right brain hemisphere.

Everything in the universe is relative and we are as one. All of us are harmoniously united with a basic essence and continuum of the cosmic.

What is deemed as negative experiences during various cycles in life does not alter this fact. As we evolve in consciousness and the veil is gently lifted, this truth is 'ever becoming.' A key in returning to the positive stream of vibration is love. It is the binder that sustains our working relationship with laws of the universe. Love that is given in an unselfish manner will eventually return in a manifold nature and affect our entire being. Become aware that the cosmic loves us and we are a necessary part of it, for without this truth we could not experience this moment in time. Through meditation we will find the spark of cosmic love in our heart. Then let it grow to a flame within and magnify it further by radiating its light toward all life, here on earth and beyond. Love is creative and eternal; it can never be lost, only ignored. As its golden light surrounds us, it will illuminate our path that leads to peace profound.

The thing to remember is that prayer is not meditation. Though prayer can be comforting at times, it is basically plead bargaining that centers on our ego. When the ego becomes involved in this manner, true meditation becomes lost.

There are those that parade around professing that they have found the ultimate perfection of spirituality, in lieu of the fact that half of their lives are literally spent hiding under a table from a fictitious Satan and the other half is spent praying to the Old Testament god, Jehovah, who believed in genocide and the stoning of people to death Is this called living and what we were put on earth for, to worry and fear? Is this not an insult to the Divine Mind's essence of love?

PEACE

(Is peace nothing more than an ideological myth, a frail imaginary structure that resists even the smallest gain)

Peace is a comforting word that symbolizes serenity, harmony and love. People in many lands celebrate the yuletide season with the theme of peace on earth and goodwill toward all. This is great, but why is such a positive attitude well nigh forgotten for the rest of the year? What is the reason that makes it so difficult to maintain this spirit for a longer duration? Is it merely a dream or an illusion to our sense of reality?

It must be first realized that concepts of peace are based on our personal evaluations and the scope of it may vary with each individual. The differences are contingent on our experiences, levels of reasoning and particular needs. From this standpoint, the odds of two impressions coinciding completely with one another remain remote. So, from the beginning we have a myriad of discordant images of the word that is supposed to exemplify harmony.

Are we deluding ourselves into believing it's possible to mix all mental conceptions of peace into a homogeneous consensus and still expect an epitome of success? Is peace nothing more than an ideological myth; a frail structure of the imagination that resists even the smallest gain? Do indications strongly suggest that we are led down a primrose path and lulled into expecting a utopia in full bloom at the other end?

History proved that efforts of attaining peace in a mass accord either failed miserably or endured only for a short time. The biggest weakness appears not in motivation but in the idea it can be objectively activated from a singular concept. Morality is most difficult being legislated to any great degree even within nations, as this would be posturing bias standards to the extent of endangering free opinions and options. Moral convictions prove anti-productive because they seldom have open ends. For refined knowledge or new data to be accepted, flexibility is a must, as growth and progress depend on it

The impetus toward peace is a soul reflection but we often shy from acknowledging it because of false imagery that religions have conveyed on true spirituality. Could this desire for peace spring from the fountain within, where a higher level of existence was once experienced at some other time or place?

Hoping to achieve suitable progress toward world peace, we cannot use obsolete methods of sharpening swords for intimidation and control. No one can rationally force their concept of peace upon another and then expect to engender the same. Yet, this madness continues every day in various ways and degrees of magnitude. Wars are constantly fought in the name of God, country or any other excuse that eases our conscience. We are so shortsighted and adamant in our own ideological concepts that the logic and respect of other views are largely ignored. This also relates in poor judgment of our actions and the consequences that later befall us. It's very important to realize and accept factors in their truest light; to do otherwise, only erects more barriers against future communication and understanding.

Waiting for peace to cross our threshold while we still bear ill will against our neighbor, is a paradox. If we are at peace with ourselves in the subjective sense, then it will be objectively visible by the love shown toward others. By recognizing peace as a personal concept, we are better prepared to understand and respect varied ideals. It is also necessary in knowing that what we believe in, is neither pristine nor absolute. These attributes reflect wisdom likely beyond our grasp and not yet attainable in our dimension. The depth of comprehension to any actuality evolves in relation to comparative knowledge and our existing level of reasoning power to analyze it.

If allowances are not made for refining our various concepts then we are not progressing in an effective or natural way. When dealing with the abstract, if there is no progression then regression is taking place.

In such a case, there is no static condition, only an arbitrary passing point between the polarities.

It is indispensable to reconcile and compensate for differences when possible. Peace as a condition is in a constant state of flux and as such it is most difficult to stabilize, much less control. Thus flexibility and constraint is required to offset its undulating nature.

Of highest priority, too, is the need to understand and know one's self, for unless this is achieved there can be little success in establishing a relative rapport with other humans.

Peace of any sort cannot be manifested until the universal essence of cosmic love becomes a personal reality in our heart and demonstrated by the way we live. In other words, we must walk the talk, not only in the treatment of others but also in the respect and amiable co-existence with creatures in our environment, as well.

Lip service is not enough for a purpose to become actively alive. Peace will never become a reality if we shirk our responsibility to act wisely. What happens when we allow others to make decisions that will control our lives? Are all the wars and suffering during the last century trying to tell us something? Depending on guidance from external forces has so far been non-productive. Look what has happened to our water, soil and air in the last two centuries. If there is a desire to better the world for our children and heirs to be, it must begin with determined involvement to maintain a healthy and productive environment. From a logical viewpoint, no fit person comes into this worldly realm without a responsibility or it would not necessitate their being here.

When our actions become more positive, cosmic love will then rise accordingly, magnetically attracting these vibrations in others and adding to its power. As this force continues to grow, no army or dictator would be able to stop it, for only the conditions of peace will be acceptable for ushering in the earth's new age.

TO OUR GOOD HEALTH

(To relieve stress, a method of diminishing anger must be used to protect health and keep from overreacting)

Until the middle of the 20th century most ailments of the body and mind were treated separately. Both medical and psychiatric professions were struggling with cures while neither was aware of the correlation there was between many diseases of body and mind. As time passed and more advanced testing equipment became available, diagnostic results showed a greater degree of accuracy in the experiments conducted. One important discovery made was that if certain chemicals were lacking or too abundant within our bodies, it made a difference on how the brain functioned. Why this wasn't realized before when they saw a drunk staggering down the street is a moot question. Now, by the use of drugs, minerals and vitamins to maintain healthy organic balances within the body, many ailments are cured or in remission.

All of this became a 'foot in the door" to many other discoveries. Not only did chemicals improve health conditions, electronics have now entered the field. Our bodies are formed from trillions of electrons and it's only common sense that such a complex system would develop a short circuit now and then. Doctors admit they don't heal us and can only assist the body in healing itself. It's logical then to assume that this assist can also happen with properly applied electronics, here and there.

For a number of years, body areas were treated by acupuncture, acupressure, manipulations, massage, x-ray, etc., to alleviate various health problems. Some practices dealt directly with nerve centers called ganglia, which is an integral part of the body's electrical wiring system. A new study in progress has obtained excellent results with only minimal help from practitioners, drugs or electrical appliances.

It is becoming more evident that mental attitude and positive thinking have a definite bearing on numerous factions of health.

This concept proves once again that the whole entity must be taken into consideration and a balance achieved through mind, body and spirit. Traditional ideas made an individual practice out of all three instead of using them in a holistic manner. The spirit portion of this trilogy was largely ignored in the last century but what alchemists have known in past ages is finally being realized. More physicians have recently recognized the value of natural cures and are experimenting now with some past age remedies.

For countless centuries various family, tribal and national cultures nurtured prejudice and biased opinions of their day and these were then inherited by following generations. These negative traditional thoughts suppressed the natural progress of societies and denied them of a higher quality of life. The twentieth century became alive with new discoveries that changed many primitive ideas and some concerned our health.

Though diet and exercise is essential, attitude also proved to be a necessary ingredient for the optimum of wellness. Thoughts with strong emotions can be stressful and affect our health in a psychosomatic way. Anxiety, hate, depression, etc., can weaken our immune systems, causing vulnerability to a variety of diseases. Anger, worry or stress that lasts for over a few minutes has a negative effect on the heart, our organs of digestion and the entire glandular system. The reason behind this is that certain glands secrete fluids for a fight or flight situation when we are strongly agitated and if the hormones are not used up they become toxic to our bodies. When this is repeated too often, stress will weaken our glandular support and take its toll in heart problems or other areas that may affect both physical and mental conditions.

Dwelling on the negative too long can create a chain reaction that attracts our thoughts to similar situations and eventually bring on severe depression or trauma. This lowers our vibratory scale and resistance to all sorts of bad bacteria 'waiting in the wings' for a chance to feed on us.

A good idea is to devise a method of reminding ourselves of diminishing anger as quickly as possible and to keep from overreacting. If counting to five does the trick before we reach ten, so much the better. Pinching ourselves or slapping the forehead with an open palm might also do the trick. Most any method is fine if it reminds us to cool down and look for positive alternatives. If answers are not immediately forthcoming, we must not become impatient for that too will only add to additional stress. A certain amount of stress is necessary for most types of development but nervous stress for any duration can be detrimental to our health. It is best to put an unsolved problem on hold when possible, giving an answer time to mature and having faith in a favorable outcome.

In any case, should mistakes be our fault, we must not let the guilt overwhelm us for this can be very devastating to good health. Think of it in this way, that perfection has yet to be invented and error belongs in an educational category. We might look for humor in small 'boners' and view larger miscues as necessary examples. For big mistakes, apologies could be in order and confessions may help too but not in front of certain close relatives or more stress might automatically develop. Last on the big list, a recompense of some sort may be necessary. After that it must be visualized as disappearing down a drain.

It cannot be overestimated what mental damage fear can do, for it is like a dark cloud hovering over us filtering out all positive light that is beneficial for growth and progress. Fear is a chain that binds us from being our designated selves and allows others to control us. It saps our confidence, kicks responsibility 'down the stairs' and we wind up losing self-esteem. When setbacks are looked upon as necessary experiences they are much easier to overcome and we can then function on fruitful efforts of improving the situation.

If we frame our minds for additional guidance, meditation is the key for obtaining cosmic data that can influence our decisions.

First of all, mythical fear must be pushed aside so we are free to think for ourselves. It is important to use free thought as we mature so it becomes an integral part of determining our destiny; otherwise, lessons in life that were allocated only for us, will remain on hold indefinitely. It's also important that we surround ourselves with positive thinking people and distance ourselves from constant gossipers and complainers.

This does not give us an excuse to go out and immediately shoot a favorite in-law, however. In such a case, it may be wise to wait a day or so and be sure to check the legality of such an act in the area in which we live. There are still some backward communities where recycling of this nature is considered to be 'not nice.' Most negative folks are usually firmly rooted anyway and trying to change them will create friction and breed contempt, plus a possible feedback of thumbing their nose at us.

A common mistake among couples is trying to remold a partner after marriage and this often winds up sleeping in bed with an enemy.

Of ways to support good health, one of the best is that of successfully dealing with stress. Slapping heads to suggest 'cooling it' can also have a down side if one has a short fuse; for abundant anger could result in the loss of an eyebrow. It is best then to get permission from loving spouses to belt them across the forehead until the other one heals up.

Lack of communication is a 'big downer' and may lead to 'popping pills' that causes even bigger problems. It is best to confide in a trusted friend and then start talking our 'head off, so long as it is put back before dinner or we may starve to death. Seriously, we should all have, at least one good friend who will listen to our problems, besides the family dog.

Should pain or lack of sleep become a problem, we must be very selective in our choice of medicines for many have serious side effects. The most important step we can take when medical ads appear on TV is to hit the mute button. Of those in one poll, 97% agreed that one little push on a TV remote could save nearly 500,000 lives in the next year or so. The other 3% were found to be working for the drug cartel.

OUR HERITAGE AND FUTURE

(We are the embodiment of swirling electrons and with this knowledge many doors were opened up)

During the early A.D. centuries, Christian religion grew into an organized power touching nearly every facet of life. It was an effort then as it is now, to control people with a common concept of the Divine. To strengthen their positions, they preyed on pagan superstitions of people and with fictitious threats of eternal damnation, it further added to their insecurity. Their power was absolute in many countries when the rulers became converts and then forced their beliefs on their subjects. People that were disobedient or noncompliant to the church's concepts were dealt with severely and often put to death.

The Christian Reformation stripped some of this power from the mother church but its movement conformed to many decadent practices of that era and many still do. It merely split the power and became self deceptive in numerous ways. Within the last few centuries science grew in recognition and many new discoveries were made that challenged the roots of most religious concepts.

One important step forward was the empirical proof concerning energy factors. By photographic means, the energy emanations seen by so many people for ages, was finally verified. As all things are made of electrons, it encouraged further research and scientific experiments that covered the whole spectrum of the mineral, vegetable and animal world.

Though human auras were always sensed in various ways, few people had any knowledge of their implications. It is now generally known that even colors in auras have an impact in their immediate surroundings.

Colors not only give clues to mental and physical conditions but they also contribute to psychic feelings between individuals as well.

Few of us are aware that most humans are constantly competing for dominant energy strength over others. Though it may be subtle at times, this deception has been an underlying influence in all marital disputes and cause for a majority of civil disturbances both small and large.

The yen for power and control may be personally orientated or it can escalate into group forms as well. Our obsession for winning in sports and the impetus to be number one in most things is a prime example. It is no wonder there is so much friction in society and we live in such a state of bewilderment. A logical solution is to neutralize inharmonious conditions but this would be complex when dealing with mixed causes.

A recent survey went on to show that most behavior was accrued from family and childhood experiences. Some of it appears to be copied or inherited in a cellular manner, much like animal instinct. It becomes then, a gene pattern for following generations, the chain of which is not easily broken. One good example is an abuse factor that is commonly referred to as a second birth order syndrome. Other abuses that relate to alcohol, food, sex, etc., can be acquired from earlier influences also.

This one study went on to say, that the majority of character traits formed during our childhood years fell into four categories.

For ease of recall, let's frame the first letter of each to spell ADAM.

A.- Aggressive and intimidating.

D.- Disagreeable and questioning.

A.- Aloof and secretive.

M.- Martyr and sympathy strategy.

Although these categories appear to be quite valid we often forget that there are always positives and negative polarities relative to any manifestation. A problem we have with most discoveries is that the strongest impressions received are usually from the negative side. Now when aggressiveness is used to accomplish worthwhile tasks, it would be functioning in a positive mode and this too must be considered with the rest of the listed traits, as well. Some of these ADAM features may give us an edge that otherwise would not be available to us. If used discreetly and no harm is done, we could be better off than trying other methods that might cause friction, hate or retaliation of some sort.

Though we may drift in and out of different categories at various times one will usually remain dominant. Applying these categories to actions of family and friends, this system is reported to be quite accurate in the majority of times.

On human behavior, problems are sure to follow when excesses or extremes become a dominant factor and these are usually caused by selfishness or lack of moral constraint. Blaming others for the adverse situations can also be self-defeating; for these circumstances may have been to benefit higher purpose. How we deal with responsibility reflects on the polarity levels our character is operating from. Motives benefiting self along with others will foster the most positive results. Here again, it is attitude that becomes the key in determining our progress.

A good start is to think well of ourselves for we are basically good people with small problems and a few of us with larger ones. There is sound reason to believe that intuitive influence from past lives may be partially responsible for some things we now experience. However, our immediate concern should center on efforts to correct or control present situations, if possible.

It is in our best interest to take advantage of mental and psychic tools that were in place long before psychology became a trend. When there is an important decision to be made, intuition can play a significant role. More attention should be given subjective impulses and let them develop naturally within our thought processes. Dreams can be helpful too when dealt with properly. Most of them jump randomly between objective and abstract thought and make very little sense. Dreams, none-the-less, are part of our mental process and that state is also subject to our influence. Before falling asleep, the subconscious can be directed not only toward a desired subject but to its recall as well. By continual practice amazing results can be produced. When we are not yet fully awake, our brain operates between Alpha and Theta wave lengths.

Frequency ranges contained therein are conducive to the meditative state. The casual focus on something during this dream state may give us the relative import or answers that carry over into our waking state. This procedure is effective with either past, present or future events.

The psyche, like the cosmic, does not recognize specific time factors and is the reason so many seers who attempt it, winds up with a 'foot in their mouth.' Once in awhile they may be correct but more than all else, it merely exemplifies the odds there are in guesswork.

It is expedient though to analyze larger objective events that happen to us for none of them comes our way by chance. Given a free will, we have choices on how to react on certain things. The right decision then, can successfully eliminate a negative feedback now or at a future date.

Often, the meaning behind events might not be clear to us at a given time and because of this, anxiety and fear of the unknown prevents pursuing the path that reason dictates. In complex situations, seldom are answers immediately forthcoming and in most cases, steps must be taken to reach a proper decision. Results usually speak for themselves and although we may not like what is eventually revealed, they have cosmic purpose and are meant to be. Personally implied tasks should not be taken lightly.

It is difficult to appreciate our position in life if we do not strive to use it wisely. Excessive attention given to lesser things obstructs our vision to more important tasks that can be achieved. Just as rain drains away, destructive thoughts must also pass from us. By sending forth vibrations of cosmic love to others, not only strengthens their energy fields but will benefit us also, for the action of love is reciprocal.

The key to keeping the gift of cosmic or divine love within easy reach is 'don't leave home without it.' As the emotion of this love is multiplied, its power can accomplish miraculous things and when it becomes a personal reality, our spirit will no longer be limited to this plane on which we now live. This can be our future.

MOMENTS IN OUR COUNTRY'S PAST

(If we have lost those rose colored glasses for awhile, let us then take a peek into the murky waters of reality)

At present, too many of our civil strengths are being used negatively, An example; Money used for science and engineering to develop quick and more destructive ways to kill one another is sheer insanity. For the preservation and economy of life, this wide spread horror must stop. If huge business profits from war were no longer tolerated, these conflicts would all come to a screeching halt. How long will it take for us to grow up mentally and emotionally? Are we too fearful to think for ourselves and only feel secure following a crowd?

Most of our downfalls are the result of 'hurray for me' attitudes while we ignore consequences to others and our social responsibilities that are the extensions of family life. Let us not appease egos into the belief that we are a civilized society. Not until the "I' is replaced with the 'We' and our viewpoints come with a caring and sharing attitude, will we be able to function as a family in peace with one another.

Every day we see a breakdown of conscience morality in people when excess materialism becomes a dominant factor. They act like wild predators with no concern for even their own ilk. Greed and selfishness has always been strong points of uncontrolled capitalism.

Patriotism for the good of country and its citizens appear foreign to their vocabularies. They seem to hate all workers that belong to unions and are striving to break them one by one for they want complete control and cannot rule as a 'de facto' dictatorship while there are still opposing views.

True spirituality cannot grow where excess materialism becomes a dominant factor and seeking answers to worldly problems from religions is a 'no-brainer' for it has proven to be the biggest cause of friction since their inception. Teaching that theirs is the only true belief, they are thus condemning all others as false. This is prejudice and a base for bigotry that turns into friction when dealing with others.

Does this not point to religion as a school for hypocrisy? Religious leaders are losing ground on moral issues, so they dream up crusades made up of false facts. On the abortion issue they exaggerate that this is responsible for the murder of millions of children and babies. The fact is that not one child or baby has been killed by abortions. A child has to be a baby first and a baby must be born outside the womb to be considered one. How can it in any way, shape or form be decided as murder when a fetus attached to the host body has yet to be born outside of that body? For whatever reason, fetuses have been removed for over a hundred years. If believing like zealots that God is in control, are we going to be so stupid as to accuse God of murder in the event that some woman has a miscarriage? Think about it this before we let some false prophet make a fool of us. If we desire to speak against murder, then let us join crusades for peace? This would save thousands of the living from actually being killed or blown to bits and maimed for life. Is it cowardice or ignorance on our part when an issue is made about hypothetical murders of fetuses; then to turn around and support daily atrocities of war for profits gained by corrupt warmongers? This or any other country is only as great as the wisdom of its leaders and should they take us down a path to infamy then all our flag waving is nothing more than a propaganda ploy. Desecrating the flag by symbolizing our loyalty to presumptuous causes is hypocrisy. Insecurity of this type belongs in a schizophrenic category or is it okay to kill anyone on suspicion that they might have a gun in their pocket and could use it on us. It's bad enough wanting to change our constitution, now we have a leader who gives the golden rule a new meaning, 'do unto others before they do it unto you.' Hooray, for the progress of our civilization. It is break out the flags again, boys, for there is a new batch of recruits to convince that war is glorious and they are much better off as dead heroes in this war than to survive and have to fight in another one against the Chinese communists.

All because some wealthy patriots back home are swiftly shipping jobs out to support the largest communist population of the world. It is sad to think that thousands of G I s were killed and wounded in Vietnam.

Ironically, that war was fought to save our country from being overrun by communists and now we are playing 'footsy' with the regimes who are taking jobs away from our working people.

The most patriotic thing we can do to save the lives of our service personnel is to recall all troops from foreign soil. We have no business to be there and try to force our ideologies on others. False pride should not overrule common sense for this is not a ball game where somebody has to be declared a winner. Lost lives, suffering and prolonged misery of entire families are at stake. Those uprooted back home now number into untold thousands with no end in sight. The human cost of foreign lives and destruction of their lands should be things of concern too, for they all have family feelings and attachments. For better or worse, let other people choose their own destiny and how they wish to be ruled.

Our president is desperately looking for something to compensate for his failed decisions and this is a dangerous situation because he is not a rational thinker and as before was influenced by a gang of unqualified people in his cabinet and elsewhere. Everything to date has backfired.

People out of work are losing their homes, cars, etc, along with small businesses going under or being lost to hostile takeovers. Also affected are lowered profits of businesses that still must operate in this country. All of this came about in the name of capitalism, the uncontrolled and glorified system that is liberal only to the rich. There is still much doubt among many what a symbol of conservatism actually means unless it is conserving the status quo that portrays an unchanging position or that of standing still. This may also reflect on negative factors like conserving greed or totalitarianism. More can be understood about earlier thought and their motives by browsing through historical records.

From the historical data gleaned it is quite apparent that capitalism and communism are much alike in totalitarian respect and even now radical capitalists are trying to limit the freedom of speech. It is questionable why we are considered a democracy with our freedom of speech when the only way the average worker in this country could be heard was by writing to congressmen who did little about anything that went against the status quo. Our legal system was British copied and although the system was improved over the years by England, the U.S. dragged their feet and was more Puritanical than anything else, where nearly always it favored invested interests. The unions struggled to represent the 'blue collar' workers and got higher safety standards, better wages, improved benefits, etc. We have heard a lot of flack about paying good wages to someone who had one unskilled job of tightening bolts all day. So what, perhaps he may have been a handicapped veteran who fought in one of our wars and this in the long run would not really matter, because every dollar he earned was put right back into our economy. His money in numerous ways helped to support education, public services etc. This is what democracy is all about, when operating properly we feed off one another and thus it becomes a reciprocating system where everyone has more equal benefits Unions helped stabilize the concept and it worked very well with a majority of cases until capitalism got complete control again. After most good paying work was shipped out to other countries, it is now back to lower pay, sweat shops, unsafe working conditions and elimination of humane benefits. It would not be surprising to see these predators try to overturn the child labor laws next. And why not, did they not get away with it by using foreign child labor without batting an eyelash? It would do well for us to stop chasing 'butterflies' and realize that a capitalist is like a predator that is born without a conscience. But unlike an animal predator that eats until full, a human predator having adequately sufficed itself will begin hording with no end in sight.

They appear to believe our resources are up for grabs regardless of an inherent responsibility to the environment and other life forms, be it humans or otherwise. When wealth becomes excessive it creates power and the ego expands along with it. This usually induces a kind of insanity where they dominate and intimidate like uncivilized bullies. An example is the hostile takeovers of smaller companies. Politicians still sanction this type of robbery. A person starts out small working his 'tail off' and putting in excessive hours until his business has grown quite successful. Big business then notes that profits of the smaller one is now worthwhile taking over and then starts their 'steamroller tactics' to acquire it. The capitalistic concept of free enterprise stinks because they can restrict the freedom of others to seek the same level that they themselves now have. Small businesses were America's backbone at one time until the cusp of the 20th century when the industrial revolution changed all that.

For a long time after, many immigrants who filled these jobs were treated worse than animals. Factories back then had very few safety restrictions, no injury compensation and the length of time worked each day often coincided with daylight hours. There was no overtime pay and on Saturdays the workers were granted a short shift and were let out an hour or two earlier. If a worker had a serious injury or lost a hand, he was sent home and immediately replaced by another immigrant off the street. (Is this is why immigration laws are ignored today?) The injured worker received wages for only the hours worked that day, had to pay for his own doctor bills and was seldom hired back, because he was now considered handicapped. In this respect earlier slaves were treated better than later immigrants for slave owners had an investment in them and when sick or injured they were cared for to get them back to work.

There were no child labor laws back then either and it was no great surprise that our country was one of the last industrialized nations to pass laws prohibiting child labor.

Some of the things witnessed by the older people who lived during that era makes one wonder why this country was deemed so great; or had the word civilized been completely ignored? Even children 10 to12 years old were allowed to work in the factories and at quitting time it was common to see some coughing and spitting blood in the snow. During winter months with factory windows closed, the air pollution in some places must have been horrible. Having growing kids work long hours without fresh air and sunshine would be devastating to their health. Many of these poor youngsters trying to earn a small pittance to help their family out were already in the final stages of tuberculosis which back then was fatal disease and a diagnosis of it was usually too late to save the person.

Immigrants like the slaves made this country rich but none realized much reward for their efforts. The predators through political power took full advantage of both natural and human resources and even during WWI these brave patriots paid others to take their draft number and fight their war for them. Not only did slaves make their owners wealthy but their homeland was robbed of resources by Europeans and shipped to the motherland, which added to that nations wealth, also.

Very little respect was given inhabitants of other lands and with a shipload of soldiers, its skipper had only to stick his country's flag into the ground where he landed and thus claim whole territories in the name of his king or queen and some of this land covered thousands of miles. Like the law of a jungle, this appears to be the same mindset as today's human predators. Many still have a mistaken notion that we are a highly civilized people. But how can this be, when we continue to sanction war and try to intimidate others with 'bullyboy' tactics?

Many shy from discussing the negative of anything but if it appears to be true, so be it, for only then can improvements be made to offset it.

If a pitfall is ignored we are apt to find ourselves in it repeatedly.

Once elections are over, the weakness of our government lies in its lack of expertise within political parties and it soon becomes a quagmire. Cabinet members on down are appointed to new responsible positions with limited or no experience before hand. So now we have a complex government being run by amateurs with no other qualifications other than the merit of being a party member. So long as we have lobbyists running around with bags full of money furnished by special interest groups, we have lost the credibility in government functions to run a democracy efficiently. To illustrate this we have only to look at the opening of the St. Lawrence Seaway to the Great Lakes. All the best experts on environment, ecologists, etc. and their opinions were either ignored or never asked by politicians because of negative influence the lobbyists had on our statesmen. Thus the most important decision in history affecting the purity and management of our Great Lakes went down the drain, as it were. We all know the impact made over the years by alewives, lampreys, zebra mussels and other species foreign to our fresh water that were allowed to enter and threaten the environment of not only the Great Lakes but also the rivers and streams that emptied into them. Fishing industries were not only ruined by the natural traverse of sea creatures but also from foreign ships as they emptied fluid from their bilges that carried with it dangerous species of fish, uncontrollable weeds and more pollution into our drinking water. The burden of expenses that were involved to save our Great Lakes and its waterways eventually fell on the state and country taxpayers. No retribution or penalty for those responsible for violations were given or seldom considered because the freedom of enterprise and capitalism was determined foremost and this had been a propaganda mindset in place for many earlier generations. We have over twenty percent of the earths surface fresh water literally ruined in the last one hundred years by poor government decisions of catering to the forces of capitalism and ignoring data from the experts.

This is just one of numerous 'boo boos' that were made by the 'good old boys' from the country club set without relying on expert data that is usually available. Lobbyists and pork barrel should be cast aside when decisions of this magnitude are to be decided upon.

Little forethought is given to how quickly things can change and when a bad decision is made how irreversible or costly a correction can be. Permission of illegal immigration is another example. Intelligent and responsible people do not reproduce like rabbits and than dump the surplus off for neighbors to support. The opposition to birth control is the religious stigma of trying to make a reality out of mythology and this concealed hoax is passed on to unsuspecting followers. There are many other negative factors that overpopulation can create and this is covered in an earlier chapter.

No matter how much effort is spent trying to be positive from the things we have learned, there will always be failures from time to time.

After catching ourselves in error and then analyzing it briefly it becomes apparent that we knew better but for some reason its importance eluded us. What was thought to be a negative attitude that had been erased from our memory track came back to haunt us. It proves that once a thought becomes habitual it is very difficult to eradicate and how vulnerable the human mind can be to its influence, quite possibly for the rest of our lives. This must not discourage us from continuing toward our goal for the lesson is well learned that nothing or no one is perfect.

Though practicing tolerance when dealing with others, it should also be rendered unto ourselves. Human consciousness is destined to grow rapidly and because of this; religious mythology will fade into oblivion.

Various facets of science too that would include revamped medical research no longer tied to drug companies; will literally explode forward as it seeks universal information through the Knowledge of One.

However, why stop there? There is always room for improvement in the predominantly positives also, for nothing is static and everything moves progressively forward. That is why we must remain mentally flexible and alert to possible changes. Our minds are like 'baby diapers' and if they are not changed once in awhile, we may be burdened with some old smelly attitudes.

Some may find it difficult to accept any validity in the principles of reincarnation and for varied reasons it is not something to be force-fed on another individual. Many things were mentioned about it before, but it would not be accepted if fear remains a factor with the doubter.

Two other things may make a difference to those still living on the cusp. If problems still have no justifiable answers when traditional thought is used, try applying the principles of reincarnation and if this makes more sense then we have a key to unlock many other problems.

Very recently, there have been experiments conducted by Dutch and Russian scientists that give this principal a boost and also verify out of body experiences from those that were once pronounced dead; plus more physical proof we really have souls after all. We need additional information and more research before this can be substantiated but with new technologies it is not unusual for important discoveries to surface rapidly. To keep an eye out for more data, we might consult Internet, magazines and other media sources. This could be a hot item and if true could blow a lot of holes in traditional thinking.

Although we are given the keys to further progress, it is still up to us to unlock the door and find the reward that awaits us on the other side.

CONCLUSION

(If we can best know self through reflection of others, is it not wise before passing judgment, for us to make sure of forgiving ourselves?)

We hope our journey through the discourses was enjoyable as well as enlightening. What was discussed is really not alien to our minds but merely viewed from different perspectives. The more facets of anything that is examined, brings us closer to clarifying an actuality of truth. The lack of intelligence may not be a factor, but when adhering to traditional concepts that are regarded as near perfect, the growth of our awareness capabilities become stunted. Most of us are usually unaware that this problem exists and more logical study of actions, personal or otherwise is needed before we can adjust to this reality. A lapse in time may be favorable under certain conditions so we can prepare adequately for a transitional change. With an exception of masters and avatars, we are still on the bottom rung of our 'comprehension ladder' looking up. Only becoming adept at memorizing what was taught us is just a small part of intelligence. The brain has two hemispheres and if both portions are not in position to analyze incoming data correctly, we are prone to thoughts of others and are not self-thinking people. As such, we unknowingly may promote errors and pyramid ignorance that would be detrimental to future generations and their societies.

From a rational viewpoint, we can never treat universal purpose in a singular manner, for it must be a continuing interaction between life and its environment. Unless there is recognition of our unity in the cosmic that renders respect and love for all that is, then any action opposing this will have negative repercussions felt personally or by many others as well. Remember, that inaction has an effect also, the severity of which would then be related to the degree of irresponsibility that is involved. Example: A tragedy happened today because a 'watch out warning' was not spoken by a witness. Does this leave the witness free of any guilt?

It must be remembered that a universal law of cause and effect was in place long before humans decided that they were holy enough to speak for the Divine and then created illusions out of personal superstitions. Taking hearsay as a truth before examining the polarities involved is presumptuous and self-defeating.

This type of action will bring judgment upon self and produces a negative backlash that may affect generations to come. As all things are relative, motives must be questioned or we are apt to be easy victims of innuendo and propaganda. Everything in nature evolves along with that of our consciousness but logically, only the Mastermind of the universe can know the absolute of anything.

What capacity we have to think and analyze is a cosmic gift that should be put to good use. Disuse or misuse of this wonderful attribute would desecrate its purpose and could be the gravest error of our lifetime.

To progress naturally requires flexibility and adaptability to positive discoveries and the consistencies of change. Outside of proven sciences, allegiance shouldn't be pledged to any specific idea unless it is realized to be of a temporal nature that may have to be compensated for at some future time. To keep an open mind, posture ourselves in this manner, "Yes, I believe this for now but will opt to change my mind if something is demonstrated to be of far greater value or closer to a perceived truth." This is difficult for most because our security demands perfection, which is just another mental illusion. As myth becomes habitual, pride resists admitting to error or accepting any improvement to its rigid beliefs. A common mistake is to rely entirely on answers from outside sources without questioning relative factors. We should pay attention to our intuitive wisdom or practice meditation that is channeled through the Soul Internet and produces finer results. In opposition to this action, others attempt to organize biased thought into a common denominator; some of which carry slogans that cater to bigotry and fear.

Most of these concepts engender traditional bias and any progressive ideas are abhorred and ignored. This type of mindset usually projects ideals as perfect and this may take many generations before sensible adjustments are recognized.

We are on the world cusp of a wonderful new spiritual age. Before this era matures very far, there will be many earth changes in the making and for us to be a viable part of it, will take varied ongoing commitments and changes as conditions continue to fluctuate. Should the polarities of earth, sea and air slowly become unified, it is quite probable that our 'Mother Earth' having served her primary purpose, will then adapt to a higher level of dimensions Of the billions of planets in our universe, the odds of this happening to some are more than just conjecture. As this factor magnifies; prejudice, greed, hate and power aspects that are so active now, will be dissolved, for this negativity would be unacceptable to the world's new nature. Those with a proclivity toward these things could no longer exist within the new earth's realm. There will not only be a huge recycling of the earth's physical nature but its inhabitants as well. Studying this manuscript can be beneficial and help prepare us for an uncertain future; so we may be able to handle what has to be done without confusion and fear of the unknown. With intuition more mature we have a better chance to work with confidence as help from the cosmic continues to guide us. Becoming a viable part in the earth's transition can prepare us with experience needed for greater cosmic responsibility. When our growth reaches a certain point, progress will become virtually unlimited. What is revealed in this manuscript is merely an outline but we now have the keys to open the door for further enlightenment. To fill in the blanks of anything that is not clear will take 'homework' that can only be accomplished by the individual; for the strengthening of personal growth is our own responsibility and the ultimate reason we are here.

Let us not question why things seem more difficult for us to achieve than some others, who seemingly appear to get all the breaks etc. etc.

Could it be that they are further along in their progression and at some time or other have eventually passed the test that we are just beginning to face? Many things can be responsible for what may seem inequitable but we should not dwell on them and increase our negative burdens. A humble attitude and avid desire to learn are the only requisites for us to cross into a new frontier of awareness. Once on the path, things will continue to be revealed, at a pace best suited for us. Personal energy and knowledge should not be given to those who are ill prepared for it. It is useless to explain Einstein's theory to someone who is not yet adept at studying math. Causing confusion or stress to another's comfort zone, usually fosters fear or hate and only creates roadblocks to their rate of personal advancement. Those that read this book are usually prepared for new knowledge but it is natural for some to move more slowly with portions of it. Though the path to a higher consciousness may be very gratifying, there are always challenges to overcome but it is natural that all worthwhile goals must be earned. There will be times when we lose attention of family and older acquaintances but much more pleasurable relationships will be formed as we travel with others on the same path. The closet place of Divine spirit resides in the soul and searching for its truth cannot randomly be found elsewhere. Our soul is the 'lock box' that holds our personal contract with the Creator, as it were. We don't need religious tug of wars to tell us how and where mythical gods can be found or contacted. If God is a spirit of love that is eternal and our soul, being a part of that Divine essence, must also inherit that longevity; for energy is never lost, it only changes form. If our progress is successful, we may not have to come back to witness miseries that are now endured.

Prayer need only be a sigh of thankfulness for cosmic acceptance. No matter what approach is taken on prayer, if it has a personal comfort effect, then this is a positive factor. Prayer has good points like humility, confession and repentance, but loses much as a pleading tool, per se.

Meditation and prayer are not the same, for the ego is always a factor in prayer. What is considered plea bartering in prayer may be worthless and perhaps an insult to a Divine Creator. Can any rational person actually believe an omnipresent Spirit does not know what we need, want and/or deserve?

Should prayers like such be pursued, we may as well be talking to a brick wall. In fact, many people in Jerusalem still talk to a wall. There is an allegorical story of a man who prayed before this wall for years with no sign of any being answered. Then one day while praying before the wall, a loose stone fell on his head and a voice from above spoke out to him.

It said, "Go home, Samuel, and mind the store, for a stew is burning on the stove and the goats are eating your straw mattress!"

Most extreme religious concepts border on falsehood and propaganda. Other than an authentic place or name, if the rest of the story cannot be verified, it becomes a mere assumption and should be treated as myth or fiction rather than fact.

The following examples –

One –   Holy Bible (fiction) "holy" is an unproven human conception.

Two –   Bible is God's word (fiction) only written by man who said it was.

Three – God spoke (fiction) human hearsay, no proof God ever said a word or that anyone was given authority to speak for the Divine mind.

Four –   Writer inspired by God (fiction) and being in a Divine 'ballpark', only our Creator of the universe could make such a decision. Is it not odd that for some reason, God is still not talking?

We must be tolerant of other people's misconceptions for it is human nature to desire immediate answers and strive for perfection. This then relates to our feelings of insecurity in whatever it is imagined to be and find it difficult to realize or admit that knowledge was withheld from us until we were capable of handling it.

Freedom of thought is a two-way street with entitled flexibility, until a time of reality, for instance, when we cross into the wrong lane with a semi-truck bearing down upon us. At this time, an illusionary faith in miracles and that God is in control will not save us. Only by turning the steering wheel with our hands can this be done for these are the tools our Maker gave us to use.

Though not always aware of it, we are responsible for our problems but can take steps to remove personal barriers by using our Soul Internet for this is the pipeline to realizing our destiny.

Like small children, let us seek the light of love in other eyes, blend it with our own and radiate this power to all that surrounds us. The joy of living will return again as once it was when our soul's birthright was first fulfilled. An aura of love shall bless and protect us as we journey onward into the new millennium.

There has always been confusion to some about the proper procedure for meditation. The more thought given to this, the less inclined we are to believe that rigid methods are foremost. We know that concentration and contemplation along with visualization is necessary but whatever it takes with intonations, music, etc. in subduing ego awareness is essential for success, also. Transferring subject matter to an intuitive area requires slowing down vibratory conscious levels so that objective awareness is not likely to cause meditation interference, just as static blurs out radio reception. A basketball will not go through a hoop automatically nor will success in meditation come without practice and coordination. Be assured though, that if our attitude is proper, what knowledge is needed will not be denied us. Waiting time varies and answers are not always in unison with our anticipation but what is best for us shall be.

One mystical adage relates that our temple must be properly tiled before the inner sanctum is approached. Contrary to most illusionary supplications devised by human minds, a line of communication with Divine intelligence begins with the soul.

This gift of soul stems from the essence of our creative Source and is the closest line of communication we have with the power of the universal mind and this is accomplished through meditation.

The basic meditation formula works much like this,

Self unto soul will speak --- Soul unto Cosmic will seek ---

Cosmic unto Soul will reveal --- Soul relates to objective Self.

Any contact with Divine or Cosmic wisdom also increases harmony, love and power. At times, answers will be forthcoming without an entire meditation procedure. This is rare and some self-proclaimed adepts then become overconfident when this is personally experienced but later 'fall flat' when they depend on it.

All realities have two sides that also contain certain anomalies and determination of successful conclusions relates to accuracy in evaluating them. Perfectionists often reject the whole because of minor points of error which would be much like 'throwing the baby out with the dirty bathwater.' Why over re-action is still a prevalent weakness with the supposed intelligent societies of today, is an ongoing situation that will keep psychologists busy for quite some time.

Satisfaction in seeking the truth is that of finding errors and being able to correct and improve portions that need to be corrected. Truth, per se, is an absolute factor that cannot be added to or detracted from. The biggest problem is our inability to perceive truth in its entirety. Depth of truth must coincide with the level of consciousness and when there is no progress in this area, the ego is left to defend the many errors of misconceptions. Anything based on repetitive hearsay requires very little thinking and because of this, the brain's analytical ability declines. Therefore our awareness of a truism, must then take a seat 'at the back of the bus,' as it were. Awareness must involve both brain hemispheres and include relative thinking but all of this is usually alien to minds that tend to gravitate toward traditional or religious dogma and try to defend myth and fantasy as a truth, even though proven to be a perpetrated hoax.

Over population, pollution, wars and resistance to factual science can all be traced to mythical systems. Christians like to preach love and peace but historically condone greed and wars. This deception endured for two thousand years so must we now continue to pass this insanity on to future generations? If peace has not been diligently strived for after losing our loved ones in a war, must we bear the guilt for having them die in vain? If they could come back and ask why we are still fighting one another; what might our alibi be? Would we be a hypocrite and pass the fault onto others? What was done to promote peace or demand accountability from elected officials? No conflict is ever won if either side has lost a son!

By accepting the various traditional views, we give charlatans power on morality issues and put our trust in corrupted politicians to run our country. Regardless of imperialistic thinking, this country's resources belong to all citizens but political manipulation of laws favor capitalism. The conservative party of greed has finally sold our country out to big business predators who want to create an economic dictatorship with their grand design of robbing the world's natural and human resources for their own insatiable greed. Those that cannot see this happening are sometimes referred to as the backward folks who want to keep up with the same direction in which our country is now heading.

Common people have the power of changing our world, personal or otherwise, for the better. It begins by becoming more vocal in our public affairs with discussions, petitions and voting. If these rights are not used we will lose them. Vote out of office all who supported the warmongers. Everyone must know that the terrorists of 9/11 were Egyptians not Iraqis and destroying their beautiful cities and killing untold thousands of men, women and children was totally unjustified. We must seek change in our government and this must be pursued in a peaceful manner. Find a better way for competitiveness by improving the lives in this country as well as the world. Only in harmony, can our civilization rise to continue.

Some history about the author –

Enlisted during WWII – July in 42 and discharged April of 46. Nearly 3years of this time was spent on active sea duty that touched on 3 continents and 10 trips escorting convoys. During this time, the contact made with various people and cultures greatly changed his attitude on many things in later life.

He chaired numerous negotiating committees when a blue collar worker and because of equality views he was black balled a communist, even though none of that stuff was ever studied.

Served several terms as a Lodge Master and also repeated stints of Secretary and Treasurer.

Have three accredited patents but never expanded on them.

Wrote ten poems – most are copyrighted.

Learned to play a mountain dulcimer upon retiring and recorded four songs, none of which made the top ten or fifty for that matter. The only excuse for this, he says, is that Kenny Rogers and Anne Murray were pre-occupied at the time and thus missed out on becoming famous.

He wrote many articles that appeared in the local newspaper.

Also, delivered original discourses at lodge and public meetings.

Roasted honorees at their retirement parties.

Was called upon to speak at several ship reunion banquets, too.

Personal note – My life has been very fulfilling and I am ever grateful for support of family and friends and the other beautiful people that made it all worth while.

Yours sincerely,